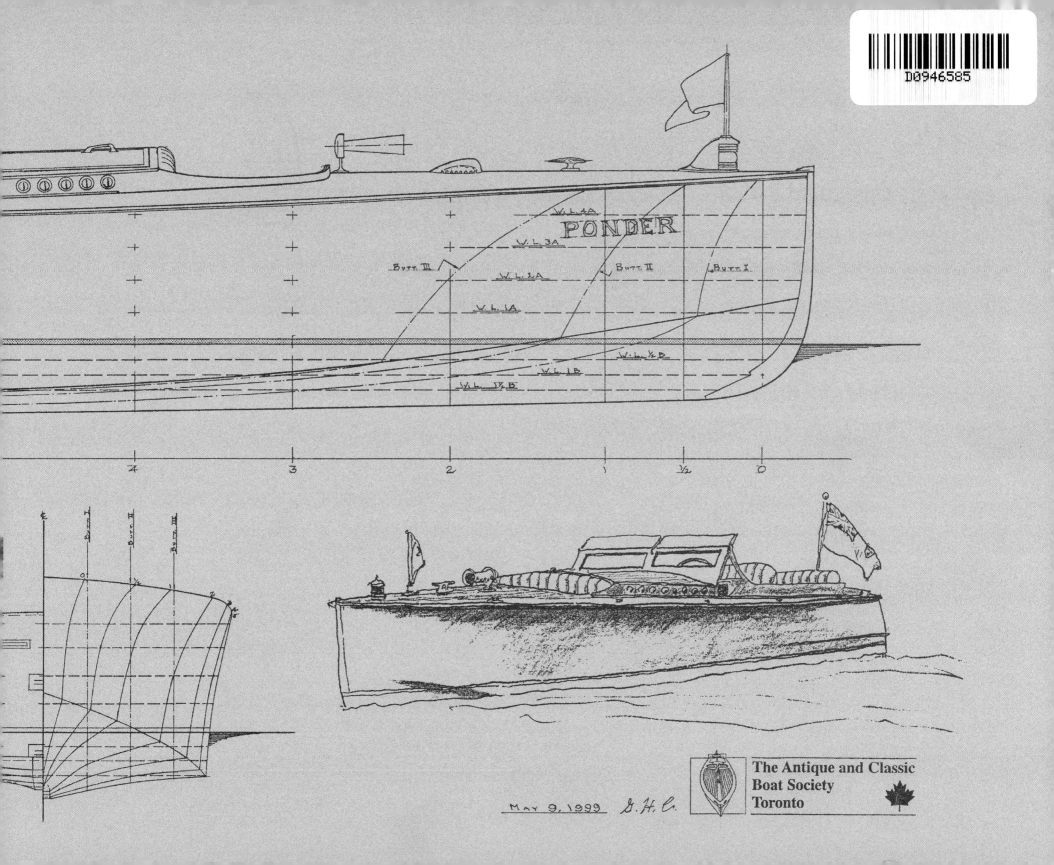

PONDER

W.L.4A

V.L.3A

Butt III   W.L.2A   Butt II   Butt I

W.L.IA

V.L.½B

W.L.IB

W.L.½B

4   3   2   1   ½   0

Butt I   Butt II   Butt III

May 9, 1999   G.H.C.

**The Antique and Classic
Boat Society
Toronto**

DITCHBURN
A MUSKOKA *Boats* LEGACY

DITCHBURN
Boats

A MUSKOKA LEGACY

HAROLD SHIELD   ♦   BEV McMULLEN

The BOSTON
MILLS PRESS

A BOSTON MILLS PRESS BOOK

Published by Boston Mills Press, 2002
132 Main Street, Erin, Ontario N0B 1T0
Tel: 519-833-2407   Fax: 519-833-2195
e-mail: books@boston-mills.on.ca
www.boston-mills.on.ca

In Canada:
Distributed by Firefly Books Ltd.
3680 Victoria Park Avenue
Willowdale, Ontario M2H 3K1

In the United States:
Distributed by Firefly Books (U.S.) Inc.
P.O. Box 1338, Ellicott Station
Buffalo, New York 14205

07 06 05 04 03   1 2 3 4 5

CATALOGUING IN PUBLICATION DATA

Shield, Harold, 1928-
Ditchburn boats : a Muskoka legacy / Harold Shield ; photography by Bev
McMullen.

ISBN 1-55046-412-4

1. Boats and boating--Ontario--Muskoka--Pictorial works.
2. Ditchburn Boats (Firm)--Pictorial works. I. McMullen, Bev
II. Title.

VM321.52.C3S55 2003   623.8'202'0971316   C2002-900929-4

Book design by Tiffany Pelka and Susan Darrach, Darrach Design
Printed in Canada

CONTENTS

KEMAH II

FOREWORD

Although sixty-four years have passed since the last Ditchburn boat left the Gravenhurst factory, their products continue to set the standard for the glory years of wooden pleasure-craft construction in Muskoka. Survivors are treasured reminders of a time when craftsmen built boats by hand, using the finest materials, creating a custom product uniquely suited to its purpose and its owner.

The final collapse of the company in 1938 was a calamity for many people—the workers, the community, the boating public, and especially Herbert Ditchburn, the genius who had guided the company to its domination of Canada's boating industry. Progressing from simple fisherman's rowing skiffs to luxury cruisers of 100 feet in length, Ditchburn products had penetrated unexpected markets in New York, Montreal, and Western Canada, far from their home waters.

Today, as we try to make sense of a world that is changing dramatically, these wonderful reminders of the past have assumed a new importance—reminding us of the impact of beauty, function, design, integrity, and craftsmanship on our daily lives.

Synthetic materials, mass production, and standardized design largely replaced traditional wooden-boat construction after the Second World War, but the desire to maintain the beloved products of the Ditchburn Boat Co. is increasing each year. Owning a vintage wooden boat has become a status symbol as well as a pleasure, and is now also a responsibility.

To Canadians, the importance of preserving the remaining examples of Ditchburn production is clearly demonstrated by the zeal and dedication of Ditchburn owners. Fully aware of their special status, they have devoted time, money, and skill to maintaining these important vessels, and they have been generous in sharing their good fortune by cooperating to the fullest extent in the production of this volume. Through their efforts, we may share the glory of Ditchburn excellence for many years to come.

We Canadians are famous for our modesty, often the last to recognize that some of our products are indeed world-class. In the first three decades of the twentieth century no pleasure-craft builder anywhere surpassed the Ditchburn Boat Company.

A NEW FRONTIER: A NEW HORIZON

The Canadian history of the Ditchburn family commences with the arrival in Toronto, in 1869, of four brothers—William, John, Henry and Arthur—who had been attracted by the government offer of Free Grant Land for settlers in the newly opened Muskoka area. This forested wilderness, which begins about 100 miles north of the city of Toronto, marked the southern boundary of the geographic region known as the Canadian Shield and was still sparsely populated. Theirs was not a happy introduction to the frontier.

A fifth brother, Thomas, the eldest in the family, had also journeyed with them to Canada, but accompanied by his wife and six children, he left the group at Port Hope, where a more secure farming life was available. Boarding the ship *Dacia* at the Victoria Docks in London on June 17, 1869, the twelve family members endured a rolling passage to Quebec City. William wrote, "We are not very comfortable in our cabin but it is only for a short time so we have resigned ourselves to our fate."

Muskoka is a land of lakes—over 1,600 of them, mostly small, but all studded with islands, with rocky shores covered with pine trees. Today it has become a vacation paradise, but to the settlers of the late 1800s it presented an uncompromising battleground, requiring a constant struggle to survive. The dense forest cover dictated that the first industry would be lumbering. However, used to the gentle, rolling farmland of England, most settlers despaired of taming this rocky wilderness.

William also wrote, "I have been to the Muskoka District where the Free Grant Lands are situated but it seems to be the opinion of everyone here that they are very dear as a gift as the land is very rocky and barren and the cost of clearing is very great.... This life would only suit a hardy Canadian or one acquainted with the backwoods and invulnerable as to mosquito bites, and ready to do battle with the black bear."

Having grown up in the upper middle-class surroundings of St. John's Wood, a comfortable part of London, the Ditchburn brothers were raised as English gentlemen. Thomas, their father, had been a lawyer; their grandfather, John, a manufacturer of ropes and cordage at Gravesend. Henry and Arthur, the two youngest, had sailed around the world as midshipmen. William had received some training in an architect's office, while John had been apprenticed to a marine designer in Brighton. None had sufficient experience to be deemed qualified in these professions, but even their limited experience was to prove useful in the near future.

Their mother, Emily, daughter of a wealthy family, had died at an early age. Then their father passed away in 1860. Each son inherited a modest fortune at age twenty-one, but a few years later this money was mostly spent or lost in unwise investments. Poorly equipped to earn their living in England, they made the decision to emigrate to Canada together to seek their fortune in a young land.

Misfits in pioneer life, not completely trained for any profession, discouraged by black flies, mosquitoes, and the rocky, tree-covered land, they returned to Toronto, where they proceeded

This carefully preserved "passenger's contract ticket" to board the ship *Dacia* on June 17, 1869, shows that full fare for the twelve family members was 59 pounds, 10 shillings. Daily water allowance and weekly food ration was carefully listed. Ten cubic feet of luggage space was allocated for each adult passenger. Although it was not exactly a Caribbean cruise, they did arrive safely at Quebec City.

to exhaust all other career possibilities. However, in September of that same year they made a second attempt to embrace northern frontier life, travelling to their land grants at the village of Rosseau, then little more than a shoreline landing place. Three large and interconnected lakes—Muskoka, Joseph, and Rosseau—form what has today become an expensive vacationland, with the village of Rosseau situated on the northernmost shore of the most easterly third lake.

Getting there from Toronto in 1869 presented a considerable challenge, as roads were merely bush trails, railroads mainly followed the shoreline of Lake Ontario, and wayside inns provided only the most rudimentary accommodation.

From Toronto, the brothers were able to take a train to Belle Ewart, on Lake Simcoe, then a steamboat to its northern terminus at Washago, and finally a horse-drawn stage to Gravenhurst at the southernmost point of Lake Muskoka.

In June 1866, Muskoka pioneer A. P. Cockburn had launched the *Wenonah*, an 80-foot side-wheel steamboat, at Gravenhurst, and she was soon sailing daily to several points on Lake Muskoka, including Bracebridge, Beaumaris, and the Indian River, below the rapids at Port Carling. While roughly built of whip-sawn planks, she certainly presented a welcome sight to tired travellers such as the Ditchburn brothers, arriving on the first regular stage service from Washago to Gravenhurst (which Cockburn had also inaugurated). Cockburn was to devote the rest of his life to improving the economy of the district with his Muskoka Lakes Navigation Company.

Confined to Lake Muskoka by the rapids of the Indian River, the *Wenonah* transported the weary brothers to a landing near Port Carling. A 5-foot differential in water level and two major rapids separated them from Lake Rosseau, and the new locks were not to be completed for two more years, in December 1871. There was, however, a rowing skiff that made thrice-weekly, 14-mile trips from Port Carling to Ashdowne Village, near Rosseau. The catch was that, as well as paying the ferryman, passengers were expected to row part of the way! It was thus that the four brothers arrived to start their new life on the frontier.

A survey crew had established a wilderness camp in nearby Cameron's Bay, and here the travellers found help and advice in a friendly backwoods setting. Exploration of their land grants, combined with their recognition of the hopelessness of clearing the bush to become farmers, left them overcome by despair. So a new plan surfaced: they would purchase the supply boat in which they had arrived and go into the transportation business.

With muscle power and an added sail, they brought in food, building supplies, passengers, and mail. For two summers they supplied the survey camp and other settlers. But their business was to be short-lived. Before the Port Carling Lock was completed and in operation, the *Wenonah* was warped up the rapids of the Indian River by building a series of temporary cofferdams, and once she was on Lake Rosseau, the steamship quickly captured the available transportation business. However, her owner, Mr. Cockburn, was already working towards providing additional business opportunities and employment.

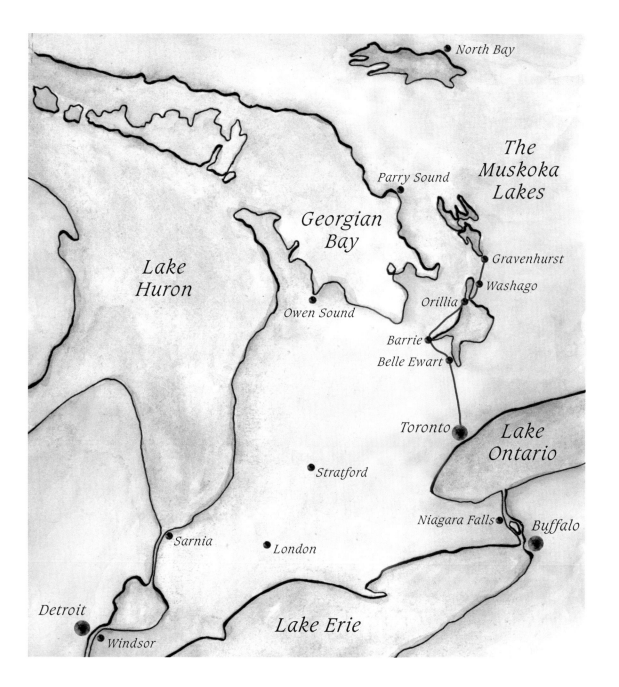

Cockburn hosted an energetic and shrewd American, Mr. William H. Pratt, of New York City, on a tour of the lakes, and Pratt immediately recognized the tourism potential of this beautiful wilderness. If visitors could be assured of enjoying all the comforts of home, he thought, they would pay handsomely to vacation in this remote area. Part of the appeal would be the thrill of travelling to an unspoiled frontier location, and once there, the natural beauty of the location, plus the abundance of fishing and hunting, would ensure a memorable experience.

It was easy for the Ditchburn brothers to fit into Pratt's organization, and William became clerk and bookkeeper for the flourishing new hotel. This employment soon led to his becoming township clerk and postmaster of Rosseau. Meanwhile, the other brothers had begun building rowing boats in the upper storey of the house that William had built for his family. It was apparent that these boats would be required in large numbers,

The Muskoka territory begins about one hundred miles north of Toronto. In 1869 it was not an easy destination, requiring rail, steamboat, and stagecoach transportation.

15

Thomas Joseph Ditchburn

A famous ancestor who pioneered iron hull construction of steam-powered vessels including the *Fairy*, built for Queen Victoria.

The family of brothers could boast a distinguished maritime heritage in the person of Thomas Joseph Ditchburn, a somewhat distant relative, who had been born in Chatham, England, in 1801. Educated locally, he was entered as an apprentice in the Royal Dockyard there, where he distinguished himself in his seven years of work and study. On leaving Chatham, he worked for a London firm that had achieved some fame in the construction of iron vessels powered by steam engines.

Entering into a partnership with Charles Mare, Thomas Ditchburn won a contract from the Russian government for the construction of a small iron ship, the *Inkerman*, which was used with great success against pirates in the Crimea and the Black Sea. Relocating to Blackwall, the company, now known as Thames Iron Works, became famous as builders of both iron and wooden vessels. By 1844, due to refinements in his hull designs, T. J. Ditchburn had achieved a remarkable 18 mph in some of his iron-hulled, steam-powered vessels.

In all, over 500 vessels were constructed in his career, the two most famous being the *Fairy*, a Royal Steamship built for Her Majesty Queen Victoria in 1845 and propelled by an Archimedean screw, and the *Volna*, an 1848 iron schooner yacht for Grand Duke Constantine of Russia.

as on-the-water recreation was the main interest of the vacationers. By 1875, the Ditchburn family was in the boating business, albeit with modest vessels of simple design.

A. P. Cockburn continued his developmental efforts for the Muskoka Lakes District by encouraging another entrepreneur, Hamilton Fraser, to build a luxury hotel at the northern end of Lake Joseph, duplicating the success of Pratt's Rosseau House. The new Summit House offered splendid accommodations and a first-class dining room. Both hotels attracted a loyal clientele, with guests coming from the United States, Canada, even Europe. They were housed in opulence and surrounded by crystal chandeliers, expensive wall hangings, luxurious rugs, and fine furniture. Fraser named his location Port Cockburn in honour of his friend, and the steamship *Wenonah* delivered guests to each hotel from the new rail point at Gravenhurst.

To capitalize on this expanding business opportunity, the Ditchburn brothers decided to divide their forces, with William and John operating in Lake Joseph serving the Summit House, while Henry and Arthur would continue at Rosseau.

A boat-building shop was built on Rosseau Bay, where boats were both rented and sold. John continued to build boats in his brother's Rosseau house, taking them to Port Cockburn for rental.

Both businesses flourished, and rental liveries were soon established at all the major resorts on the lakes: Rosseau, Port Cockburn, Port Sandfield, Port Carling, and Windermere. The rental fleet now numbered in the hundreds. Young workers were recruited and trained, and production increased to meet demand. One of these trainees was Herbert Ditchburn, Henry's nephew and second son of William. Energetic, organized, and quick to learn, he proved to be the successor that Henry was seeking, and the man who would build the company into a major Canadian boat-building enterprise.

Summer visitors were increasing each year, and it became obvious to Henry that the Muskoka Wharf at Gravenhurst, where the Grand Trunk trains now arrived, would become the centre of future tourism and development activity. Here, by 1900, he had established the site of the new Ditchburn Boat Factory, where a much larger future awaited.

Herb Ditchburn, age fifteen. Pencilled on the back of the photo is "First trip to Toronto."

Apprenticed to his uncle Henry, young Herbert soon became the principal person in the boat-building company.

Chapter Two

ON THE MUSKOKA WHARF

This was a most advantageous business location, since private cottages were springing up all over the lakes, and every cottage needed at least three boats. Canoes, sailing dinghies, and rowing skiffs were basic, but now motorboats were about to make their initial appearance.

Above left: The Ditchburn livery station was conveniently located at the shore end of the newly built Muskoka Wharf, where passenger trains delivered vacationers to the waiting steamships.

Below left: The first boat-building factory in Muskoka was erected next door to the livery station.

Gravenhurst's first boat-building plant was erected immediately adjacent to the Muskoka Wharf, right where the new railway line delivered passengers to the waiting steamships that now plied the three lakes. Trains proceeded the length of the wharf so that luggage could be transferred directly to the steamers. This was a most advantageous business location, since private cottages were springing up all over the lakes, and every cottage needed at least three boats. Canoes, sailing dinghies, and rowing skiffs were basic, but now motorboats were about to make their initial appearance.

Private steam launches of various sizes, several of which are still in existence and owned by members of the Toronto chapter of the Antique and Classic Boat Society, had been serving wealthy cottagers for some years. Personal steam yachts had existed in both Britain and United States for many years, and two commercial steamboat ocean crossings had been completed by 1838. In Canada their use had been mainly as commercial transports on rivers and lakes, yet by the late 1800s several private steam yachts were plying Muskoka waters, joining the working fleet of A. P. Cockburn.

In 1890, Senator William Sanford of Hamilton commissioned construction of the 68-foot *Naiad* by Polson Iron Works of Toronto. With her elegant, black-painted hull and her interior trim of bird's-eye maple, mahogany, and teak, she provided ostentatious transportation for almost fifty years. Two later steam yachts—the 1903 *Rambler*, at 73 feet (now diesel-powered), and the 1915 *Wanda III*, at 90 feet—still survive, as do the much smaller *Constance* and *Nipissing*. Steam-powered yachts were sophisticated, silent, and reliable, but they were also expensive, required much of their interior space for machinery and fuel, needed at least an hour to build up a head of steam, and, worst of all, required a licensed engineer to operate them. The stage was set for the entry of the internal combustion engine, which, despite a poor beginning, was about to revolutionize the Ditchburn business.

When fire destroyed the first factory in August 1915, a second and larger building was immediately built.

No. 1 Painted Quality Basswood Board

No. 1 Varnished Quality Basswood Board

No. 1 Varnished Cedar Strip

Canoes offered easy transportation for cottagers and vacationers alike, but rowing skiffs were more popular with fisherman and soon became the standard rental vessel.

In 1904, Herbert Ditchburn, second son of William, the Rosseau postmaster, bought into his uncle Henry's business while he was still in his early twenties. Under his dynamic leadership, Ditchburn Boats grew by leaps and bounds, declaring a 17 percent profit in one year. Gains were plowed back into the business to finance the expansion needed to meet demand. The H. Ditchburn Boat Manufacturing Co. Ltd. was incorporated in June 1907, with a board of directors consisting of Herbert Ditchburn as president and Alfred Ditchburn and Thomas Greavette as directors.

Tom Greavette was born in Worthing, Sussex, England, in 1881 and came to Canada as a twelve-year-old, following the death of his father. Starting as a labourer at the Ditchburn plant at the turn of the century, he was to become a key figure in the company and a lifelong friend. Alfred Ditchburn, Herb's older brother and first son of William, was confined to office work due to poor eyesight, but he was a skilled administrator, active in the community, and also served four terms as mayor of Gravenhurst.

It would be difficult to overestimate the economic impact of the boat-building plant on the small town. Recruited locally and trained to be boat builders, the workforce was increasing every year, while at the same time the lumber industry was falling into decline. Thousands of badly needed dollars were paid to young trainees, many of whom were able to establish their own building operations in later years. Herb's practical skills in engineering, woodworking, and metalwork were constantly needed in these early manufacturing days, and even more so in the years to come, as technical advance and the rapid development of reliable gasoline engines produced major changes to pleasure boating.

The liveries at various resorts were operating to capacity, and hotel guests reserved their fishing boats as they made vacation arrangements. When a disastrous fire destroyed the Summit House in 1915, the rental fleet based there was sold to Herb and distributed to other livery stations. Herb's uncle John had retired from boat building, and all production was now centred at the Ditchburn factory in Gravenhurst, a facility that had become the largest employer in the industry.

Rowing boats of various sizes were both sold and rented from livery stations around the three lakes.

In Muskoka, the early gasoline engines seemed more trouble than they were worth. Yet there were tempting reasons to consider a gasoline-powered vessel. Rowing was tedious and backbreaking, sailing depended on a useful breeze, and steamboats were expensive to purchase and operate—beyond the range of most buyers.

Probably no one person can be said to be "the" inventor of the gasoline-fired, internal-combustion engine, but various significant developments can be traced. Dr. Nicholas Otto, a Prussian born in 1832, developed an experimental "explosive" engine in 1863, but it was not successful enough to be produced. He was later to work with a Cologne machinery designer named Eugen Langen, who was able to correct many problems, leading to a successful engine that was powered by illuminating gas. By 1877, Otto had earned patents that covered the basic principles of the 4-cycle engine—suck, squeeze, bang, and blow. By 1878, the Otto "gas-o-lene" engine was being sold in the United States and other countries.

In 1885, a tiny 2-cycle engine built by the Sintz Gas Engine Co. of Grand Rapids, Michigan, was demonstrated in a small boat. It appears to have followed the design work of a Scottish engineer, Dugald Clerk, who had patented a successful model in the 1870s.

The Steinway Piano Co. of New York had also entered the yacht-building field, and from 1891 to 1897 built a Daimler engine under licence for their vessels. With the expiration of the Otto and Clerk patents in 1895, a veritable explosion of new builders entered the market to provide gasoline-powered engines for agriculture, factories, automobiles, and boats.

European manufacturers soon included Napier, FIAT, Peugeot, and Delahaye, as well as Mercedes, the new name of Daimler. Early American builders included Olds, Simplex, Wolverine, Standard, Winton, Speedway, Fay and Bowen, Bridgeport, Victor, Buffalo, Sterling, Globe, Murray, Racine, Tregurtha, and many others.

For the first dozen years of the new century, gasoline engines were decidedly unreliable, but certain manufacturers, including Sterling, Kermath, Scripps, Standard, and Van Blerck, were soon able to dominate the marine market. But these better-quality, state-of-the-art engines were expensive. The 100-horsepower Scripps cost $3,500 in 1911, and the Van Blerck E-8 Special of 1914, which developed 220 horsepower, was priced at $2,400—more than most houses or luxury automobiles.

In Muskoka, the early gasoline engines seemed more trouble than they were worth. Heavy, unreliable, difficult to service, and needing a dangerous fuel, there were many reasons to hold off on the purchase of a motorboat. Yet there were tempting reasons to consider a gasoline-powered vessel. Rowing was tedious and backbreaking, sailing depended on a useful breeze (which often failed far from home), and steamboats were expensive to purchase and operate—beyond the range of most buyers.

In its 1908 catalogue, the Ditchburn Company expressed the drawbacks: "For ten actual years we have wrestled with the gasoline engine…and think that we have had…all the troubles that could be handed to a man with a gasoline engine. If there are any that we did not have, our customers had them, and did not hesitate to tell us about them."

Most of the very early Muskoka launches powered by gasoline were imported from the United States or purchased from builders in Toronto or Hamilton. They took the form of a small steam launch with a 1- or 2-cylinder

The 1913 *Viola* is the oldest gasoline-engined Ditchburn known to be still in service. Built as a supply boat for Captain Henry Wallace, she was used for many years on the Muskoka lakes. Now residing on Georgian Bay, she has never been restored, just lovingly maintained. The photo on the left dates to 1914.

1908: Design No. 1844 - 18 foot Family Launch

1908: The Ditchburn Hydroplane

1909: Design No. 215 - 21 foot x 5 foot Family Launch

1912: Design No. 286 - Type A - Auto Family Launch

1912: Design No. 306 - Type B - Auto Family Launch

1912: Design No. 327 - Type C - Auto Family Launch

gasoline engine dropped into the middle of the hull. A canopy top was usually added for weather protection. But as the reliability of small engines increased, more orders came to the local builders, who offered local servicing and no cost of transportation.

In 1908, Herb Ditchburn created a new hull shape, long and narrow, with foredeck, raised engine compartment, seating, and steering wheel. Planked in cedar on white oak frames, this speedster, 27 foot by 4 foot, 8-inches, was expected to achieve 14 to 20 mph with engines ranging from 10 to 20 horsepower. The hull flared outward from the keel to the shear in an "inverted wedge design," diverting spray out to the sides. Access to the engine for hand cranking was accomplished by pushing the one-piece hatch cover forward on wooden sliders. With a later 60-horsepower, 6-cylinder engine, speeds of 34 mph could be anticipated from this hydroplane.

In the next few years hull types changed rapidly, responding to the larger, more powerful engines that were becoming available. The conventional design that evolved was a displacement launch, perhaps 26 feet overall, with enclosed motor compartment, hinged hatch covers, a metal- or wood-framed windscreen to shelter the operator, bench seating for six to ten passengers, and even electric lights and horn. Electric starting motors had also made their appearance, although some vessels had an access port through the firewall to allow for a hand-cranking mechanism. Cowl ventilators were deck mounted to air the engine room; light boards for the navigation lamps were installed forward of the windscreen; and navy tops or auto tops made all-weather operation more pleasant, particularly for female passengers.

Increased power and the resulting speed placed new demands on hull design, as it was now possible to create an uncomfortable ride or even a dangerous vessel. Sudden increases or decreases of power could sometimes produce unexpected results, but the increased horsepower meant that hulls could become longer and beamier. Naval architects now designed bottom configurations, which had previously evolved through trial and error.

Gudahi, Ojibwa for "there she goes," is a brawny 35-foot launch built over the winter of 1915. Shipped by rail to Lake of the Woods, she was immediately used to carry royalty on a lake tour by Canada's then governor general, Prince Arthur, and the Duke of Connaught. Returned to Muskoka in the 1980s, she was restored to top condition and is regularly shown at antique shows by Earl and Winnifred Miller. The huge spotlight on her foredeck was apparently required for night navigation to her island home.

A unique feature is the distinctive manner in which armrests have been crafted into the cockpit coamings. A Kermath Sea Mate engine with six cylinders and dual ignition supplies power.

A disastrous fire in August of 1915 totally destroyed Ditchburn's first wooden factory building, which was then located at the Muskoka wharf. However, within weeks a new brick building was rising on the site, with greatly expanded facilities. The ruins of these second buildings still exist, although new development plans announced by the town of Muskoka will eventually require their removal.

Celebrating the new factory, a 1915 order from Sir John Eaton, the department-store magnate, introduced Herb Ditchburn to the sophistication of professional yacht design. The 73-by-15-foot day cruiser, *Kawandag II*, was by far the largest project yet undertaken by the young company. Designed by Philadelphia naval architects Bowes and Mower, and powered by twin 8-cylinder Sterling gasoline engines, and incorporating many advanced mechanical systems, this chauffeur-driven yacht must have been a daunting project for Herb Ditchburn's Muskoka workforce of thirty backwoods boat-builders.

Above: Kawandag II, the 1915 day cruiser for Sir John Eaton, was the first major commission for the new factory.

Right: The elegant bridge deck marked a new era of sophisticated controls and instrumentation.

Opposite: This lovely painting by artist Roy Davidson depicts the 1926 delivery of *Blythewood III* at the Ditchburn factory. Published by Heritage Art Editions Inc. of Strathroy, Ontario, prints are available at several Muskoka galleries.

Left: Hope II. The rare beauty of her original Van Blerck engine, a 4-cylinder, 85-horsepower model, is a feast for the eyes.

Above: When Jeff Reid became the new owner of *Hope II* he was presented with a delivery photograph of the vessel and the original owner's yachtsman's cap.

Opposite: The 1918 *Hope II* carries a maker's plate numbered 18-72. She is a 28-foot launch in stunning condition.

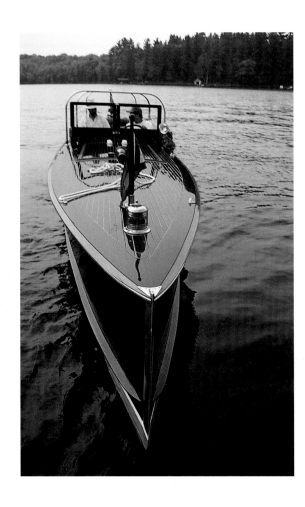

But, rising to the challenge, the company turned out a magnificent vessel, meticulously crafted of the finest materials, that was a convincing demonstration of their growing capabilities. Owned by one of Canada's most famous families, this beautifully appointed

vessel was in regular use in Muskoka until 1938, when she was sold to Detroit owners.

Other important vessels followed, including the 61-foot cruiser *Idylese*, built for Colonel Duff of Toronto in 1919. This vessel was probably the design of A. H. "Bert" Hawker, an Englishman who had come to Canada in 1907 and worked at several boatyards in the Hamilton and Toronto area before starting with Bert Minett in Bracebridge. There, in 1914, his major project had been design of the *Rita*, a 53-foot day cruiser still regularly seen on the Muskoka lakes.

Above left: The 1918 Pausar is 30 feet, 6 inches long with a narrow 5-foot, 6-inch beam, is typical of her time. Three years later this model was wider by a foot, one plank higher and a whole lot drier running.

Right: Dennis Howchin and grandson enjoy a day cruise in the 1921 *Woodwind*, a 21-foot runabout.

Always a fast boat, *B-IV* is a 1921 gentleman's racer, 28 feet long with a pointed stern. Faultlessly maintained, she now boasts the awesome power of an 850-horsepower Gale Banks Chevrolet engine. Originally built for Carl Borntraeger, she was a direct result of Harry Greening's racing success with the Crouch-designed *Rainbow I*.

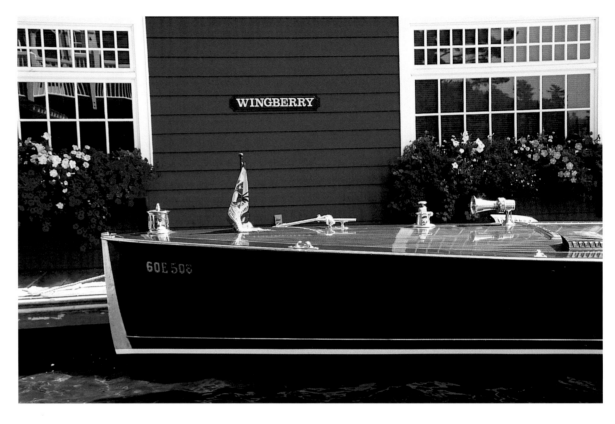

Above left: This huge launch is the 38-foot *Shirl-Evon*, built in 1921 and powered by a 6-cylinder Chrysler engine.

Below left: Struan II, an elegant 24-foot gentleman's racer, also dates to 1921.

Above right: The elegant *Wingberry* is a 32-foot launch from the same year. This was obviously a vintage year for the Ditchburn factory.

Sevlo, a 1937 hardtop launch, is the hotel boat for Severn Lodge. Built in 1932, this 37-foot utility transport has carried thousands of guests in all kinds of weather.

A Lalique crystal bird adorns the bow light of the 1924 launch *Chickadee*. Always in immaculate condition, the 26-foot vessel attracts many admiring glances, but rigging the bowlines requires special attention.

Above: Memphis Five is another 26-foot launch built in 1924, hull number 24-18. She was originally built for P. S. Stenning Coate, an American relative by marriage of Herb Ditchburn, who owned a series of *Memphis* vessels numbered *One* through *Eight* over the years.

Left: Lily, a 23-foot runabout, also dates to 1924. This was a popular model with excellent handling characteristics.

Hawker returned to Britain for service in the First World War, and upon his return to Canada signed on with Ditchburn as designer and production chief. His importance expanded with the growth of the company, his career lasting until the final closing in 1938. Both Hawker and Herb Ditchburn became versatile designers, each new project presenting opportunities for expanding their expertise and their company's reputation for luxury pleasure boats. This skill, combined with their growing reputation for quality construction and finish, soon made them Canada's dominant pleasure-craft builders.

In 1922, Sir John Eaton placed another order—for an outstanding sedan launch, truly confirming Ditchburn's pre-eminence as a builder to the carriage trade. The 38-foot *Dolly Durkin* was constructed to the highest standards. Powered by a 275-horsepower Sterling engine, she easily attained speeds of over 30 mph. With her elongated deck, raised engine hatch, uniformed staff, elegantly enclosed cabin, curtained windows, and impressive speed, she was an unforgettable sight.

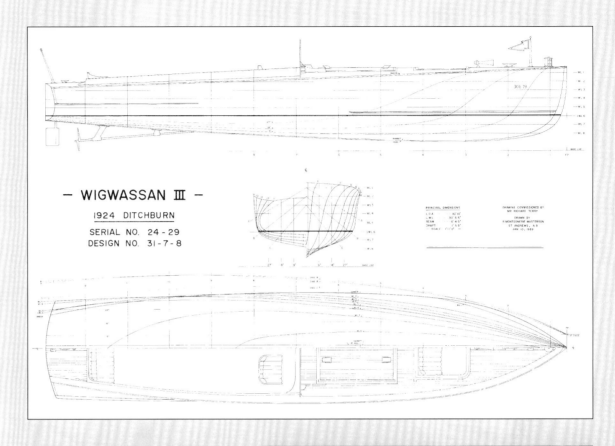

- WIGWASSAN III -

1924 DITCHBURN

SERIAL NO. 24-29
DESIGN NO. 31-7-8

Wigwassan III, also from 1924, is a 31-foot model used by the hotel for guest transportation. Owner Rick Terry commissioned the drawing of the vessel to assist in her restoration. Very few Ditchburn drawings exist, as the practice of the time was to work from a hull model and existing patterns.

These two commissions for the Eaton family were to produce many future orders from the wealthy families of Toronto, Montreal, New York, Pittsburgh, and Philadelphia.

In the early 1920s, design of runabouts and launches was standardized for more efficient production. George Crouch, professor of mathematics at the famous Webb Institute of Naval Architecture, drew the basic hull shape. This basic shape was then stretched and widened as

needed. Production was reduced to four models—21 foot by 5 foot, 6 inches; 26 foot by 6 foot; 32 foot by 6 foot, 6 inches; and 35 foot by 6 foot, 6 inches. All developed with the same characteristics, they featured a sharper V-shape and higher chine line forward than the conventional V-bottom design. The frame construction was of bent white oak. The planking was of selected mahogany with a double bottom, all flush, copper riveted with rivet heads hand drawn, filed flush. The brochure boasted, "A champion model, with a world of speed, built to last many years, these standardized boats, constructed in quantity, cost no more than ordinary runabouts."

These standardized V runabouts were inspired by the racing success of Harry Greening and the Crouch-designed *Rainbow*, a racing boat exhibited in 1920 at the New York Boat Show, where it was acclaimed as "the best runabout yet built" by the boating press. A Ditchburn brochure of the time contains a quotation from Charles F. Chapman, editor of *Motor Boating* magazine and secretary of the powerful American Power Boating Association:

Above: Ed Skinner, well-known boat restorer, leaves the Beaumaris Yacht Club with a boat load of ladies after an elegant luncheon. His 31-foot-long 1925 launch, still unnamed, is hull number 25-8.

Left: The 1927 *Duquesne*, 30 feet overall, is a consistent prizewinner at boat shows. Her engine hatch is raised to accommodate the larger engines then becoming available.

Opposite: The 1924 *Lakeview*, a 24-foot runabout approaches her boathouse.

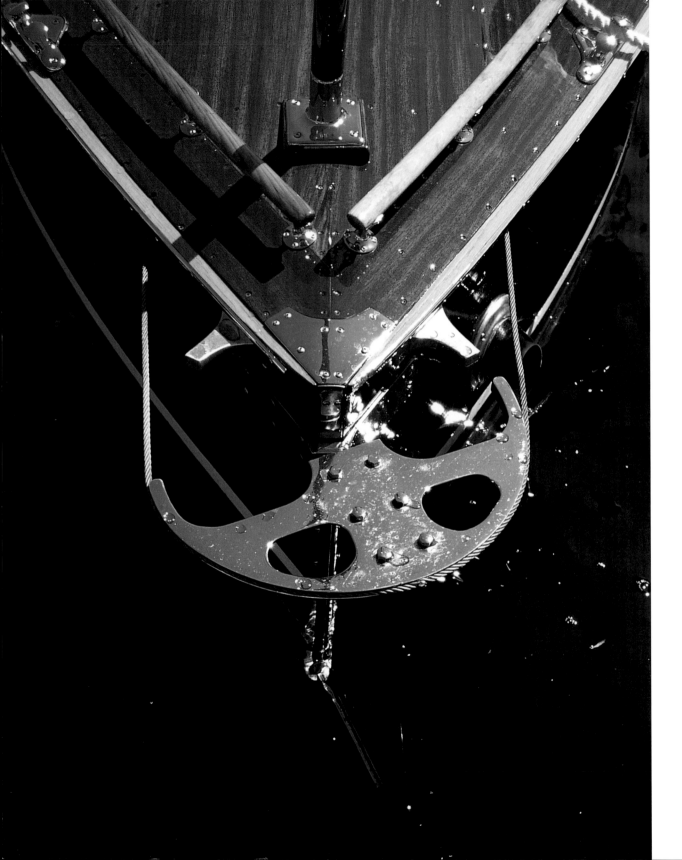

"*Rainbow*, the best runabout in the world, has again won the Fisher-Allison Trophy. Runabouts of the *Rainbow* type with similar power plants have a wonderful future before them. It is the type of boat for which the American public has been waiting long and patiently. It has been developed and perfected solely as a result of conditions governing the Fisher-Allison Trophy race, calling for a sensible, reliable, seaworthy, and fast runabout."

It is doubtful that any Canadian boat manufacturer has ever received such a sweeping accolade from a respected American editor. At that time Chapman was regarded as the dean of U.S. boating writers and was soon to be the author of the U.S. Power Squadron textbook *Piloting, Seamanship, and Small Boat Handling.*

It is also doubtful that anything more fortunate for the Ditchburn Company's reputation could have occurred than the decade-long relationship with Hamilton, Ontario, racer Harry Greening, whose international success in Ditchburn-built boats was to provide worldwide publicity of the finest kind.

Above and opposite: The 1925 *Whippet* was built as an all-out race boat and she was a regular winner in the annual Muskoka Lakes Association regatta. She was another direct descendant of the *Rainbow* heritage, 26-foot in length with a pointed stern and outboard rudder. Repowered with an 8-cylinder Crusader 410-horsepower engine, she is now faster than ever.

Below: This is what it's all about. The *Lady Jayne* sits at her dock in a quiet cove at Harraby Point on Lake Rosseau, sparkling in the setting summer sun. A very beautiful 31-foot launch built in 1925, she was first delivered to the Ottawa River. Many years later she was sold to owners in Wisconsin, then New York, before being returned to Muskoka. Completely restored to her original condition, she is an outstanding example of Ditchburn artistry.

Above left: Proud owner Bill Bartels sets out for the Antique Boat Show, where *Lady Jayne* captured the "Peoples Choice" award.

Above right: The elegant canvas auto top, premium-grade leather upholstery, special hardware, instruments, and fittings all mark *Lady Jayne* as a rare and beautiful vessel. Her original 6-cylinder Model 100 Kermath engine was also completely rebuilt.

Below left: Original fittings loaned by another Ditchburn owner were copied to replace missing hardware.

Below right: Unnamed when purchased, the restored launch was christened *Lady Jayne* in memory of a lost daughter, also remembered by a crystal angel mounted on her bow light.

Above left: Bricie is a 1926 displacement launch, 26 feet long, owned by Bruce and Marie Evans.

Above right: The 26-foot *Woodmere One* was also built in 1926 and is owned by Peter Dalton.

Right: Ron and Barbara Besse enjoy a cruise in *3's Enuff*, their 33-foot launch.

Above: This 37-foot sedan is *Blythewood III*, built in 1926 for George McLaughlin of Oshawa. She is also pictured in the foreground of Ray Davidson's painting of the Ditchburn factory on page 30. Beautifully proportioned, she was constructed to the highest standards, her hull crafted in East Indian vermilion wood. Her present owners, the Herrmann family, also own two other famous Ditchburn vessels—the race boat *Whippet*, and *Hibiscus*, a 1930 Viking.

Below left: The luxurious cabin offers comfortable cruising in any weather.

Below right: Her house flag carries the famous bear of Bern, Switzerland, in recognition of the Herrmann family's European roots.

Top left: *Highlands II* is a 28-foot launch powered by a 6-cylinder Kermath engine. Owner Gordon Wilson also owns the race boat *B-IV*. *Centre left:* The 36-foot *Robinbrook* is a Voyager model launched in 1927. *Bottom left: Bob's Toy*, owned by Robert Walker, is a 24-foot runabout built in 1927.

Above top: Built in 1928, The *Princess* is an elegant 28-foot launch owned by Lloyd and Susan Ross. *Above left: Spindrift* is a 23-foot utility model dating to 1927. *Above right: Wimur*, also launched in 1927, is a 26-foot model.

Opposite: Excitement is guaranteed in the 1927 *Dix*, a gentleman's racer, powered by a Scripps Junior Gold Cup engine. Her hull is cedar and decks are mahogany.

Robin Adair, a 31-foot launch, was delivered to the Cragg family in 1927. The photograph at left with the Beaumaris hotel in the background was taken on delivery day. Chris Cragg, grandson of the original owner, now proudly maintains this unique vessel.

Three beautiful examples of the class of '28.

Left: Tapawingo is a 26-foot model with a Graymarine engine.

Above right: La Reine, a 24-foot runabout, is used on Lake of the Woods.

Below right: Elsinore is a 31-foot launch with a 6-cylinder Chrysler engine.

The Lady Elgin, a huge livery and passenger launch, was delivered to Captain Henry Wallace in 1929. As hotel boat for the Elgin House hotel she carried thousands of passengers over the years. A dependable Kermath engine moves her at a steady 14 mph.

She looks even longer than her 36 feet with a canvas auto-top stretching over half her hull. Her cavernous, bus-like interior provides seating for twenty or more passengers. Now in private service, this well-loved treasure has been carefully restored to top condition.

Above left: The 1929 *Eleanor* is built on a 30-foot Viking-type single-stepped hull, with crank-operated side windows on the forward cockpit.

Above centre: Skookum, "Old Woman" in Ojibwa, is a restored 36-foot former hotel boat based on Old Woman Island.

Below left: Ready for family fun, the 28-foot *Mary Arden* can carry the extended family.

Right: The 31-foot *Charisma* means fun with grandchildren for Bryan and Elizabeth Rowntree.

"Awesome" is how most people describe the 36-foot *Lady Jeane,* owned by Richard and Gayle McGraw. Built in 1930, she is powered by an 8-cylinder Chrysler engine. The lower photo puts you in the driver's seat, at the custom-crafted wheel.

Above: Blank Cheque is a 1930, 24-foot Neptune model runabout. Owners Simon and Liora Yakubowicz like to share the ride with their sea dog.

Right: Areta II is a 23-foot triple-cockpit runabout built in 1930, owned by Bruce and Nancy Bone.

Brendan O'Brien, long-time owner of *Elsie*, a 1932 runabout, also writes about the Muskoka beauty spots that he loves.

Chapter Four

AT THE HELM OF A RAINBOW

Harry Benjamin Greening's contribution to power boating, his dozens of world-class achievements, his speed and endurance records, his engineering innovations, and his pioneering inspiration made him the first internationally famous Canadian in his sport.

From the unlikely home port of Hamilton, Ontario, a Canadian sportsman, inventor, and gentleman carried the Canadian flag to an unprecedented series of wins and world records, beating the best in the world, introducing amazing innovations in power boating, and gaining international honours, esteem, and respect.

In typical Canadian fashion, these momentous achievements by Harry Greening brought little recognition at the time, except in hometown Hamilton, and are now all but forgotten to later generations. In Canada's Sports Hall of Fame, an impressive wall adorned with a powerboat-racing mural carries photographs of the only four members elected for boating achievements—three men and the unlimited class hydroplane, *Supertest III*.

The three persons elected to membership are James Thompson of London, Ontario, for speedboat design; Bob Hayward, driver of *Miss Supertest III,* which won the Harmsworth Trophy for Canada; and Harold Wilson, whose many racing achievements included the World 225-Cubic-Inch Hydroplane Championship, the Silver Cup at Detroit, the President's Cup at Washington, and the World 12-Litre Championship. These memberships are well deserved: these competitors earned their way to this recognition.

But not included is the pioneer credited as "the father of motorized boating" in this country, the first to bring world attention to Canada, and the man whose *Rainbow* series of racers established Ditchburn boats as world leaders.

Harry Benjamin Greening's contribution to power boating, his dozens of world-class achievements, his speed and endurance records, his engineering innovations, and his pioneering inspiration made him the first internationally famous Canadian in his sport. This outstanding racer richly deserves to be recognized in Canada's Sports Hall of Fame.

Born in Hamilton in 1880, Harry Greening was educated at Ridley College, in nearby St. Catharines. Music was the only special aptitude he displayed, and he even considered a career as an organist before entering the family business. The B. Greening Wire Co. Ltd.

had many years of experience in metalworking and wire production, both in Canada and in England, and in this atmosphere Harry Greening was to prove perhaps the greatest mechanical genius yet developed in his remarkable family. His inventiveness and innate understanding of machinery were the keys to his many accomplishments.

Just as important were the human qualities that earned him an international coterie of friends, always willing to help or exchange ideas. Quiet, unassuming, and unfailingly a gentleman, Greening was always impeccably dressed, bringing real meaning to the term "gentleman racer."

Harry Greening was a lifelong lover of the outdoors, a boater, and a Muskoka cottager, but he was not a swimmer. He hated being cold and wore long underwear year-round. His employees represented an extended family, and their ideas, abilities, and help were cheerfully accepted in the quest for ever-greater racing success. The plant workers were given a holiday on race days, and paid double if he won.

And win he did, setting world speed and endurance marks on the water, winning gold cups and receiving rare honours beyond his own country. Imagine the odds of a young Canadian, an inventor and a sportsman, being elected to head up the racing committee of the American Power Boat Association. It had never happened before, and hasn't since, but Harry Greening's talents were appreciated by the APBA. He was also selected by the Royal Motor Yacht Club, donor of the Harmsworth Trophy, as their North American representative.

Greening began his racing career in 1904, and that career was to have a dramatic effect on the development of powerboat racing throughout the world. It also eventually resulted in Greening being honoured by the American Power Boat Association in 1953 as one of the ten pioneers who had contributed most to powerboat racing over the past fifty years.

In his first effort towards powered boating in 1904, Greening used a foot-powered lathe to build a 3-horsepower engine in his attic.

Harry Greening of Hamilton, Ontario, was Canada's first international success in motorboat racing.

Gadfly III thunders across Hamilton Harbour at 29 mph in 1917.

This engine drove his canoe at 9 mph and was a model of efficiency, so much so that it attracted the attention of aircraft pioneer and motorcycle racer Glenn Curtiss, who purchased the design from Greening after sending his fellow worker, Casey Baldwin, to Hamilton to inspect the engine.

BITTEN BY THE SPEED BUG

A series of four small boats named *Gadfly* followed this first effort, with Greening beginning a racing career in Hamilton and Toronto. American A. E. Luders, famous in later years as a designer and builder, designed *Gadfly I*. Her engine, a Model 10 Buick of about 10 horsepower, pushed her across Hamilton Bay at 15 mph— a remarkable speed for 1908. It was perhaps the first automobile engine converted to marine use. Her unjacketed exhausts burned the hatch covers and hull sides on numerous occasions. In pleasure use at Rainbow Island in Muskoka, her speed thrilled area natives, but the noisy, open exhaust caused indignant meetings among the cottagers.

Gadfly II pushed the speed record to 22 mph, with a 2-cycle, 4-cylinder, 24-horsepower engine built by Smart Turner of Hamilton. In these early days, ignition gave much trouble, but Greening solved his problems by using the new Bosch-Honald system. Actuating the spark plugs by a magnetic make-and-break system, this invention eliminated the high-tension leads that often failed because of the spray.

T. H. B. "Bing" Benson of Oakville, famous for his sailing designs, designed *Gadfly III*. The builder was Johnny Morris of Hamilton. Equipped with a 135-horsepower Niagara

6-cylinder engine, and the Bosch-Honald ignition system, she topped out at 29 mph. Only Bill Gooderham's Fauber-designed hydroplane, *Heloise*, could keep up with this speedster, and then only in sheltered waters.

In 1918, *Gadfly IV*, designed by Al Crouch, made her appearance. Equipped with a V-bottom and a 165-horsepower Sterling engine, she raised top speeds over 30 mph. Her racing career was undistinguished, but used on a "pleasure" cruise through the Long Sault Rapids on the St. Lawrence River, she ably demonstrated two of Greening's most important beliefs—that all his boats should have leather seats and carry passengers.

BEATING THE WORLD'S BEST

For 1920, Greening placed an order with Herb Ditchburn for *Rainbow I*, the forerunner of eleven *Rainbows*, seven of which raced for Canada. Designed by George Crouch and built by Ditchburn at Gravenhurst, *Rainbow I* captured top honours in the first major powerboat race ever held in North America.

Above: Rainbow I, designed by George Crouch, was the winner of the Fisher Gold Cup in Miami, winning all three 50-mile heats.

Left: Designer Crouch and owner-driver Greening exchange some performance opinions.

Rainbow maintains her lead over *Snapshot*, driven by Jack Stroh.

Thus began a decade of cooperation between Greening, the gentleman sportsman, and Ditchburn, the master builder, which was to produce fame for Canada and an international reputation for Ditchburn reliability.

Carl G. Fisher of Miami had donated a gold cup valued at $5,000, carrying with it a cash prize of $2,000, to be competed for in a race of three 50-mile heats. The heats were to be run on separate days, but teams would not be allowed to make any adjustment or repairs between heats. Fisher, a powerful American industrialist and part owner, with Jim Allison, of the Indianapolis Speedway, was tired of watching speedboats break down during races and had decided to put a premium on endurance and dependability.

Realizing that his competitors would all have about the same horsepower, Harry Greening and his long-time mechanic, Dave Reid, decided to have their crankshaft dynamically balanced. An old story now, it was almost unheard of in 1920 when Greening sought out a quirky Russian émigré to the United States who

had pioneered the technique. This technician, Akimoff, added an almost 10-percent boost to the Sterling's 300 horsepower.

Similarly, Greening wrote to Harry Ricardo in England, who was experimenting with aluminum pistons. Less than one third the weight of the originals in cast iron, these Ricardo-designed replacements were the largest built to date, and the first used for a marine engine.

Rainbow I obliterated the field by placing first in all three heats and was acclaimed by U.S. experts as the "best powerboat ever built." At the New York Boat Show of January 1920, *Rainbow I* occupied the place of honour on the Sterling engine stand, and Greening received world recognition as a racing genius.

By now, Greening was dedicated to the quest for ever-higher speeds, and he saw design change and mechanical improvement as his path to success. He reasoned that only by constant experiment and refinement could he hope to compete successfully with the much-wealthier Americans, backed by the resources of their leading industrial companies.

Holding the place of honour in the Sterling engine display at the 1920 New York Boat Show, *Rainbow I* was acclaimed "best runabout ever built."

Above: Rainbow I's engine room shows meticulous engineering.

Below: Rainbow II was not a regular winner, but important knowledge was gained from its design modifications and performance.

CONFOUNDING THE COMPETITION

Greening's next design, *Rainbow II*, was an outstanding example of his willingness to gamble—to experiment with new theories and technology. Albert Hickman, inventor of the Sea Sled, had convinced Greening of the remarkable efficiency of surface-piercing propellers, which were still very much in the experimental stage. At the same time, an American designer, Bill Tripp, had caught his attention with experiments measuring the inefficiency of propellers placed just forward of the transom.

Combining these two theories, Greening and Ditchburn designed *Rainbow II* with surface propellers and cut away her bottom planking at the stern to eliminate the vacuum caused by water rebound from her propellers. Their calculations, later proven to be almost exactly correct, estimated that if the bottom planking were carried out to the transom, the hull would carry an unseen weight of about 1,500 pounds through atmospheric pressure. This problem has since been overcome in modern hydroplanes, but at the time this thinking was revolutionary.

Greening and Ditchburn were aghast when, in her first test, *Rainbow II* would hardly move. No one had any idea of the tremendous amount of air these surface wheels would require, but recognizing the problem, they began by boring 1-inch holes just above the propellers to admit air. Eventually, they wound up with a deck opening 2 feet long by 4.5 feet wide. Every time the hole was enlarged, the boat went faster, until a speed of 60 mph was achieved. At rest she drew about 14 inches, but at speed she appeared to ride on about one inch of water.

At her debut in Buffalo, New York, *Rainbow II* was undoubtedly the fastest boat, but smashed out her bottom on a wave, sinking in a matter of minutes. She was recovered the next day by divers and her Sterling engine rebuilt in 48 hours, while the Elliot Boat Company replanked her hull in the same time. Her contribution was in knowledge gained, not racing success. Ironically, all three heats of this race were won by *Rainbow I*, which had been sold to Sylvester Egan of Buffalo.

In 1922, Greening visited Detroit to take in the Gold Cup Races, won that year by Colonel Jesse Vincent, chief engineer of the Packard Motor Car Co. Greening, realizing the advantages of the Packard aircraft-derived engine over existing marine engines, secured an engine from Packard and had it shipped to Gravenhurst, where it was installed in the John Hacker-designed *Rainbow III* being readied for the 1923 Gold Cup.

The boat proved very fast, and news of her speed in trials promptly reached Colonel Vincent. His new boat, an almost identical Hacker design, was no better than Greening's. Seeking a winning margin, Vincent abandoned his present hull, building a similar hull of much lighter weight, making extensive use of aluminum.

Greening learned of this startling development in a telegram from Hacker, just fifteen days before the race. Not willing to accept the inevitable defeat, Greening embarked on another engineering introduction—the first outboard rudder and propeller ever used on a V-bottom boat of non-hydroplane design. Ditchburn, Hawker, and Greening sprang into action, implementing an idea they had only talked about.

Placing the propeller outboard of the hull eliminated the after strut, as the tail shaft was now carried in a trunnion bearing on the leading edge of the rudder. This also eliminated the air pressure under the hull, the negative effect of which they now understood from *Rainbow II*.

Greening's own words tell the story at Detroit: "On a trial run with Colonel Vincent, he was surprised to find that while we carried four in our boat and he carried two, we were

Rainbow III surprised all competitors at Detroit's 1923 Gold Cup races, easily winning the first two heats.

Above and right: Beautifully restored by Tony Brown at Lake Tahoe, *Rainbow III* returned to Muskoka in the millenial year 2000. Owners Doug and Pam Elmore were showered with attention and praise for saving this famous competitor. Her original Packard Gold Cup engine still supplies plenty of horsepower.

about 4 mph faster in spite of his very much lighter hull and similar engine. In practicing around turns we had found that the engine would slow down from 2400 to 1500 revolutions requiring about half a minute to pick up to full speed. So we installed in the bottom of the boat a small air vent four feet forward of the wheel and 14 inches off to the starboard side. When the boat was running on a straight course, the air that went through this vent did not run into the wheel, but it did when the boat was turning, causing cavitation and consequently allowing the engine to race even over its maximum power speed. When we came out of a turn and the air was allowed to follow its original course, we came out with a racing motor, and the gains made were remarkable. Everyone had told us that cavitation would not work but we used it with very fine results as we

led in all heats, except the last, by over three-quarters of a mile."

In the disastrous third heat, *Rainbow III* broke a cotter pin on her propeller and her elapsed time on the three heats placed her dead last. Subsequently, the scoring points system was changed, making it impossible for a vessel winning two of the three heats to be defeated for the Gold Cup, but that change came too late for *Rainbow III*.

Over the next few months, Greening received over one hundred cotter pins by mail from racing fans throughout America and England, together with instructions on how to install them properly. Sheldon Clark of the Sinclair Oil Co. in Chicago marked the occasion with a gold cotter pin set with diamonds, fashioned as a tiepin, which Greening wore proudly for the rest of his life.

Sharing the cockpit of *Rainbow III* at Gravenhurst with California owner Doug Elmore, Vicki Innes, granddaughter of Harry Greening, was thrilled to welcome the famous raceboat to home waters after a seventy-five-year absence.

A WORLD RECORD FOR CANADA

After the crushing disappointment of the Gold Cup Races, *Rainbow III* was sent to Muskoka, where Greening had a much different project in mind. On Lake Rosseau, a 19-mile course had been laid out on government charts, checked by the Muskoka Lakes Navigation Company, and here Harry Greening proceeded to establish a new 24-hour endurance record. On September 18 and 19, 1923, *Rainbow III* ran 1,064 miles to shatter the existing record set by the liner *Mauretania* when she logged 760 miles at sea from noon to noon.

Charles Chapman, famous editor of *Motor Boating* magazine, came from New York not only to write the remarkable story, but to participate as a part-time helmsman. His words put the achievement into perspective. "*Rainbow III* is the first boat—power or steam—to make a thousand miles within twenty-four hours. She may have lost an A.P.B.A. Gold Cup in September by the loss of a cotter pin, but this performance has overshadowed any victory or achievement by any type of floating craft, present or past."

Despite their initial misgivings concerning such a severe test, Packard sent mechanics from Detroit to assist, but the 200-horsepower stock engine performed flawlessly. Dave Reid, Bert Hawker, and Charles Chapman shared the driving chores with Greening, with the run getting underway at six o'clock on a cold Muskoka morning.

To achieve 1,000 miles in 24 hours it was necessary to average 41.7 mph, provided no time was allowed for pit stops. Even if no trouble developed, it was felt that the 50-gallon fuel tank would necessitate stops about every 80 miles. Fuel consumption turned out to be less than anticipated, however, and refuelling stops were stretched to 95 miles. Still, this meant that no lap could take more than 26 minutes, 17 seconds, if the refuelling times of 5 minutes each were allowed.

Herb Ditchburn and Bert Hawker designed an elaborate refuelling system to get the gasoline from barrels on the timer's barge into

An angel of spray forms behind the speeding *Rainbow III*.

Rainbow's twin tanks. A large air pump charged the fuel drums, providing a sizable stream, and the system worked to perfection.

The first four laps with Harry Greening at the helm were made in 25:55, 25:25, 26:05, and 24:25. Refuelling was accomplished in 2 minutes and 40 seconds, and then *Rainbow III* was again on her way, with Dave Reid at the helm.

It was astonishing how uniformly round after round was made in the cold, windy, conditions. Despite rain on the second 12-hour stretch, this consistency was maintained, and with improving weather the test took on the atmosphere of a pleasure cruise.

Breaking all water speed records for distance between 150 and 1,000 miles, *Rainbow III* averaged 44.3 mph for the 1,064 miles, completed in 24 hours. Deducting the 32 minutes and 53 seconds consumed in fuelling stops, the average speed attained was 45.3 mph.

During the entire test, the 625-cubic-inch Packard engine ran without attention of any kind except the replacement of one spark plug. Two gallons of oil were added,

Cockpit details show the straightforward racing approach of Greening and Ditchburn.

but the engine never faltered, maintaining a steady 2,100 rpm with an occasional lap or two at 2,150. As a precaution, a propeller of smaller diameter was used to reduce engine strain.

To successfully stage such an unprecedented test of machinery and systems meant that every mechanical component had to be the finest available, designed and built to serve beyond ordinary limits. But it also required extraordinary men, dedicated to achieving the goal. Herb Ditchburn and Harry Greening were the perfect pair to pursue such an accomplishment—even if their achievements brought far more recognition in the United States than at home in Canada.

Above: The American Power Boat Association recognized *Rainbow IV's* new record of 1218.9 miles run in 24 hours with an official certificate.

Below: Hacker and Ditchburn designed a fuelling barge with pressurized gasoline drums. Refuelling took only moments.

Opposite: Rainbow IV is paced by a Curtiss Seagull powered by a Curtiss C-6 engine. Both are cruising at 60 mph.

WORLD BEATER OR RULE BEATER?

In 1924, Greening returned to Detroit with *Rainbow IV*, creating one of the biggest controversies in powerboat history. Once again he had introduced a revolutionary idea in his quest for greater speed. By running bottom planking diagonally from her keel across her bottom, Greening planned a series of 1-inch steps along the length of the hull, reducing her wetted surface to about one ninth of her total length. Another first of its kind, *Rainbow IV* became, in essence, a multi-stepped hydroplane. She also featured a pointed stern, since experiments with surface-piercing propellers had led him to conclude that a lift equal to 18 percent of their thrust would support the narrow stern.

Finalizing his concept with Herb Ditchburn, Greening had George Crouch draw the plans for the new vessel. Using the same engine as *Rainbow II*, it was 1.5 feet longer, 1 foot beamier, 33 inches deeper and a 1,000 pounds heavier. In addition, the new boat provided bunks for three under her long deck. Contrary to the opinions of the experts, *Rainbow IV*

proved faster than *III* by at least 3 mph. Score one more engineering victory for Greening the amateur, while the experts were still batting zero!

Knowing the racing rules, Greening realized he was in controversial territory, as the APBA had ruled hydroplanes ineligible for Gold Cup competition. He invited the APBA rules committee to Hamilton to view the new boat and to rule on its eligibility, offering to pay their expenses. This committee inspected *Rainbow IV* and presented their findings to the rules committee. They in turn declared the vessel eligible for competition as a clinker-built boat.

On August 30, 1924, *Rainbow IV*, driven by Greening, easily won the Gold Cup, blasting down the straightaway at more than 60 mph, leaving her nearest rivals, *Baby Bootlegger* and *Miss Columbia*, well behind.

Greening left Detroit a winner, with the applause of all. All except Howard Ross, owner and driver of *Lady Shores*, which had burned and sunk during the race. Ross protested that the clinker-built *Rainbow IV* was a violation of the design rules. After much deliberation,

THE 🍀

RUDDER

OFFICE OF THE EDITOR

9 MURRAY STREET

NEW YORK CITY

October 17th 1924.

Mr. H.B.Greening,
Hamilton, Ont.

Dear Harry:

Yours with copy of letter to Columbia Y.C. received and noted. It is just the sort of letter I would expect you to write. Some day, when you get good and sick of fooling around with a crowd of sea lawyers come over into a real game, hydroplane racing, where we have no rules and no protests and no bum sports. We go out and race and the first man over the line gets the prize.

Hope to see you at the A.P.B.A. meeting.

Sincerely,

Gerald S. White

Dozens of letters were received by Greening, all protesting APBA's action in stripping the Gold Cup from *Rainbow IV*.

APBA upheld this protest, stripping the cup from *Rainbow* and awarding it to the second-place *Baby Bootlegger*.

Letters of support for Greening poured in from every boating journal in America, and editorials in the *Detroit News* howled in indignation at the unfairness of the APBA's action, but to no avail. Greening was again robbed of a hard-earned victory.

Discouraged, but not beaten, Greening accepted the APBA's position reversal and relinquished the trophy with characteristic politeness. He was never heard to express criticism of their decision, only disappointment.

A NEW WORLD MARK

In the fall of 1925, *Rainbow IV*, sporting a new 400-horsepower Gar Wood-Liberty engine, arrived in Muskoka to improve on the 1923 endurance record. Once again, supporters and observers came from all over North America to witness the attempt.

The 1,650-cubic-inch engine was turning a propeller measuring 20 inches by 28 inches, pushing *Rainbow IV* to an average lap speed of 50 mph. Although this was somewhat slower than her top racing performance of 63 mph, it was felt to be a more desirable pace for a 24-hour test.

By the end of the two 12-hour periods on October 2 and 3, 1925, Rainbow had covered a total of 1218.9 miles at an average speed of 50.8 mph. Assisting at this new world's record were Herb Ditchburn, builder of the boat; James Galloway, engineer for Gar Wood; Charles F. Chapman, editor of *Motor Boating* magazine; A. G. "Bert" Hawker, who had supervised her construction; and Dave Reid, Greening's long-time friend and mechanic.

Rainbow IV was sold in 1926 to Samuel S. Dunsford of Concord, New Hampshire, who continued to race her until 1929. In 1932, her engine was removed to be used in *El Lagarto*, and the hull disappeared. Recently, John C. Binley had an exact replica built by Bill Morgan for pleasure use on Lake George, New York. Powered by a modern V-8 engine, she performed very much like the original.

Above: Rainbow IV easily won the 1924 Gold Cup, defeating *Baby Bootlegger* and *Miss Columbia*.

Left: An exact replica of *Rainbow IV* was built for Jack Binley from original plans. Photo by Harold Shield.

Right: First approved, then disallowed, the series of 1-inch steps of her clinker-built bottom created an illegal multi-stepped hull.

OFF TO ENGLAND

Dave Reid and Harry Greening co-operated to design *Rainbow V*, a much smaller boat at 22 feet overall, using much of the knowledge gained from the larger *Rainbow IV*. She was built especially for the Duke of York Trophy Races, to be run in England on the Thames River, from Putney Bridge to Mort Lake, and her engine displacement was limited by the rules to 91.5 cubic inches, about half the swept volume of a Model T Ford.

Greening turned to Harry Miller of Los Angeles, already famous for his Indianapolis racing cars, who produced an 8-cylinder engine, turning up 8,000 rpm and 200 horsepower. The pistons were about egg-cup size. However, no cast-bronze wheel could be found to withstand this rotational speed. In desperation, Greening telephoned Edsel Ford, who arranged to meet Reid and Greening at his Dearborn, Michigan, factory. Here, a pantograph machine turned out a beautiful wheel based on Greening's model. The pantograph machine had been working on new fender dies

HARRY GREENING'S "RAINBOW VII", WINNER OF FREE-FOR-ALL CHAMPIONSHIP OF NORTH AMERICA, LIPTON CUP, 1928, THE FIRST RUNABOUT CARRYING 15 PASSENGERS AT OVER A MILE A MINUTE. DESIGNED AND BUILT BY DITCHBURN BOATS LIMITED.

Rainbow VII, a giant 38-foot runabout, won the Lipton Cup at Detroit in 1928 carrying eight crew members.

costing more than a $100,000, but the needed propeller was given first consideration.

Dave Reid and Jack Marcer took *Rainbow V* to England, Greening and family joining them for the racing. Although they had the fastest boat, conditions were very poor—the Thames in flood, and almost all competitors striking tree trunks or other debris. No winner was declared, and one of the few competitors to actually finish was a woman, Marion Carstairs, who later became a Ditchburn client.

Harry Miller, the engine builder, purchased *Rainbow V* and raced her successfully for several years in the Los Angeles area.

THE BIGGEST AND THE BEST

Rainbow VII was the result of a reassessment by Greening and Ditchburn of the successful principles discovered in numbers *III* and *IV*. At 38 feet long, with a 9-foot beam, and powered by two 600-horsepower Liberty engines, this giant runabout could carry fifteen passengers at more than 60 mph. She was an excellent rough-water performer, and Greening

used her to win the Lipton Cup in 1928, when she carried eight persons during the race. She won three heats hands down to capture the North American Championship, her only serious competition coming from the Curtiss Aeroplane Co. entry. After the race, *Rainbow VII* was shipped to Lake Rosseau, where Harry Greening planned to set another endurance record—this one for 12 hours of running time.

Rainbow IV was sold to Samuel Dunsford of Concord, where she was a regular winner in New England-area racing. Her engine was transferred to *El Legarto* in 1932.

The Italians, financed by their government, had spent a lot of time and money on the 12- and 24-hour endurance records, but had gotten nowhere. Greening now showed the way again, cracking off 723.9 miles in 720 minutes, including all fuelling stops and crew changes. Her average running speed was 63.21 mph, and her fastest lap was 68.95 mph.

To accomplish the lightning-fast pit stops, there was now a redesigned system on the gasoline barge. With extra drums pumped to high pressure, the crew refuelled *Rainbow* with 180 gallons of gasoline in just 52 seconds.

Previous experience taught the crew to keep the engines running for the full 12 hours, as hot engines are very hard to restart. The run began about an hour before daylight on a foggy, chill October morning in 1928. Once again, the team set a world record.

Asked by a boating writer why he had taken on such a challenge, Greening explained, "It is very apparent that race boats such as *Miss America VII* and *Miss England* cannot go thirty miles wide open—something always happens. So I decided to show that a 1000 h.p. runabout is the equal of anything on earth in reliability, and that a speed of a mile a minute can be maintained with the utmost ease. Here is a craft that will carry ten people comfortably at 60 mph, is well built, practically noiseless, seaworthy, and a lovely thing to look at. No wonder I am in love with her. Perhaps there is an urge behind all this—to do one thing well. That is why I don't play golf."

THE LATE YEARS

Although he retired from racing in 1929, Harry Greening continued to build new boats, including *Rainbow VIII*, a raised-deck cruiser for Great Lakes pleasure use, and *Etude* and *Largo*, slower, all-weather performers for Georgian Bay use.

In 1934, Greening launched *Rainbow IX* at the Royal Hamilton Yacht Club, where he served as commodore for many years. Powered with a 12-cylinder, 550-horsepower, Packard-Liberty racing engine, she was capable of 63 mph. Greening intended to convert this hull to a

A winning combination of talent: George Crouch, designer; Harry Greening, owner-driver; and Herb Ditchburn, master builder.

hydroplane configuration, then attack the North American speed record of 73 mph held by *Miss Chicago*, but that never happened. This vessel, which had first raced as Packard Chris Craft, is now owned by Murray Walker of Lake Muskoka, and is regularly seen at antique boat shows.

Greening's racing career may have ended, but his love of water sports, fast boats, and Muskoka never died. As an elder statesman in racing he served the APBA, the Canadian Boating Federation, the Royal Hamilton Yacht Club, and many other organizations.

In reflecting on his long and successful career, Greening stated, "Motorboat designing is a queer hobby. The APBA rules under which we have always raced apparently leave no loophole and it is up to the racing committee to see that they are enforced. But that is only one end of the stick. The other is the man who is going to build the boat. He gets the rules, works over them for weeks and then says, 'I can do this and I can do that and yet be within the rules.'

"We are proud (or ashamed) to say that from 1922 to 1927, the constant change in rules was brought about by our building *Rainbows* that seemed to work between rules without hitting an important snag. Take for instance *Rainbow II*. The rule specified that hydroplanes were barred. We applied longitudinal planking (not prohibited) and pushed in part of the transom about 12 feet (not prohibited) at the same time, producing a hydroplane which was prohibited.

"Ten years later," he noted, "Adolph Apel of Atlantic City used all these principles in modified form to produce the fastest boats in the world." Faster, more seaworthy, and acceptable to the revised APBA rules, they nevertheless were direct descendants of Greening's *Rainbows*.

Undoubtedly, the design innovation and the inspiration provided by Greening and Ditchburn set the stage for later Canadian achievement on the water. The fortunate association with Herb Ditchburn allowed Greening to collaborate with a builder who wanted to be on the leading edge of all marine development. Together, they were able to win against the giants of motorboat racing.

Happily, two of the most important *Rainbows* have survived to be enjoyed today, at least in a manner of speaking. *Rainbow III* was sold to American owners and enjoyed a long and successful racing career as *Palm Beach Days*. Many years later, she was bought by Dick Clarke of Sierra Boat Co., at Lake Tahoe, where she and her original Packard Gold Cup engine waited until 1997 to find a new owner who would restore her to her former glory. That finally happened when Californian Doug Elmore bought the wooded-down vessel and organized the restoration. Surprisingly, very little new wood was needed; the hatch covers, badly charred from engine heat, were the only items requiring total rebuilding.

Rainbow VII, Canadian Boat, Driven 60 Miles an Hour for 732 Miles—A World Record

Newspapers and boating journals all over North America announced the *Rainbow VII* achievement—a speed of over a mile a minute for 12 hours.

In the year 2000, *Rainbow III* made her first return in seventy-four years to her home waters of Lake Muskoka, featured as poster boat at the annual antique boat show in Gravenhurst, presented by the Toronto chapter of the Antique and Classic Boat Society. Owner Doug Elmore was showered with attention and praise as he proudly chauffeured descendants of the Greening family around Muskoka Bay, passing within a few feet of the ruins of the factory where she had been built.

Rainbow IV also lives on, in a sense, as Morgan Marine in Silver Bay, New York, built a faithful replica for Jack Binley to use on Lake George. Perhaps the most unusual vessel in Gold Cup history, this planing hull, double-ended, with thirteen diagonal steps beginning about 5 feet back of her bow, was the design inspiration of Harry Greening, assisted by George Crouch, Albert Hickman, and master builder Herb Ditchburn. In building a replica, Bill Morgan was able to follow Crouch's original drawings, which had appeared in *Yachting* magazine many years after Rainbow's frustrated "victory" in the 1924 Gold Cup at Detroit.

The year 2000 was a real cause for celebration at the Gravenhurst Antique Boat Show, marking the return to home waters of *Rainbow III* after a seventy-four year American sojourn. Owner Doug Elmore of Lake Tahoe received dozens of members of the Greening family, even motoring several of them across the bay to view the ruins of the factory where she was built. A very much appreciated visitor.

TRANSPORTS OF DELIGHT

The growing reputation of the Ditchburn Boat Co., the stunning success of the two vessels for the Eaton family, the surprising achievements in racing, and the growing population of wealthy summer residents combined to overwhelm the workforce, which had almost doubled in 1923 and now needed larger facilities if greater annual production was to be achieved. Orders for larger vessels were appearing from satisfied previous owners, and now orders were coming from much farther afield—Montreal, New York, and western Canada.

On December 4, 1924, the *Orillia Times* carried the exciting news that the Ditchburn Pleasure Boat Co. Ltd. of Gravenhurst had decided to build a new boat factory on the waterfront of Lake Couchiching. This location was a natural choice, as the Orillia waterfront is on the Trent-Severn Canal system, with access to both Georgian Bay to the northwest and Lake Ontario to the southeast. The possibility of orders from Montreal and New York now became a certainty for sales manager Tom Greavette.

"Operations will commence next week, so that the factory may be ready by February 1 for the building of a large pleasure launch which the company has secured the contract to turn out. The boat must be delivered in Montreal in the early spring," stated Greavette.

This new order for a vessel 100 feet in length, with 6 feet of draught, expected to require over $35,000 in labour alone, was hardly a "boat." It would be more properly described as a magnificent yacht, incorporating all the latest mechanical advances, and built to uncompromising standards of craftsmanship and luxury. The yacht *Gannet*, Ditchburn's largest project to date, was being commissioned by a prominent Canadian yachtsman, businessman and sportsman, Commander J. K. L. Ross of Montreal.

Mayor McLean and other City of Orillia officials moved quickly to secure the land lease and institute dredging operations to provide 15-foot water depth for a distance of 200 feet out into the lake. A contractor promptly erected the steel-truss factory building, measuring

The 100-foot *Thalassa* was delivered to Chauncey Stillman of Royal Canadian Yacht Club in 1929. He served as commodore in 1931 and 1932.

40 feet by 120 feet, a local workforce was recruited, and work commenced. A marine railroad was added later to accomplish launchings from the twin production lines, and the entire waterfront end of the building could be removed for access to the railway.

The added capacity of the new Orillia plant produced a handful of orders for larger cruisers, while production in Gravenhurst continued at a record pace. Over the next seven years a succession of spectacular vessels were launched, each representing some owner's dream of the perfect pleasure craft. The customer list was equally spectacular, representing a veritable who's who of wealthy Canadian and American owners.

In addition to Commander Ross, Canadian owners included Sir Joseph Flavelle, Lady Eaton, Sir Edward Kemp, Sir Thomas White, Sam and

Left: A side cabin office on *Thalassa* exhibits the stunning quality of her built-in furniture and appointments.

Above: The dining salon with built-in sideboard and cupboard offered seating for eight.

Opposite: The main salon provided comfort and luxury for the owner's party, plus a console radio for entertainment.

Above: The open back deck on *Thalassa* featured rattan armchairs, built-in benches, and an attentive steward.

Opposite: Launched on May 15, 1928, this handsome 78-foot cruiser, christened *Virginian II*, was built for Gordon Lefebvre of Pontiac, Michigan, a vice president of General Motors. A party of thirty friends came from Toronto by train, lunched at Carter's restaurant, and then witnessed the launching while the Orillia town band played stirring music.

George McLaughlin, H. M. Tucker, Barry Hayes, E. R. Wood, George T. Fulford, C. S. Coryell, the Honourable Wallace Nesbitt, Walter Cole, Colonel Le Grand Reed, Harry Hatch, Norman Gooderham, Colonel Albert Gooderham, John Forlong, and many others.

The American owners' list was equally impressive, and included John Ringling (of circus fame); Gordon Lefebvre, vice-president of General Motors; Fred W. Haines of Detroit; Wharton Sinckler of Maine; Mrs. Delphine Dodge Cromwell; and P. D. Saylors, president of Canada Dry; Commodore Austin Perry; and John C. Hageman, all of New York, plus many others.

This clientele coming to a Canadian yacht builder was unprecedented, constituting an accolade never extended to a Canadian builder before or since. Herbert Ditchburn, with no technical training in architecture or design, with no schooling outside of Muskoka, now dominated the Canadian production of pleasure craft. His reputation for beauty and integrity had secured American commissions from owners who could have bought from any of the famous U.S. builders.

The *Toronto Star Weekly* in January, 1928, carried a two-page tribute written by its famous feature writer, Gregory Clark, tracing the astounding success of the small-town company, now the most potent force in Canadian boat building, and profiling the driving force behind its success. "He is reserved, even shy. He has a navy look—short, ruddy-faced and blue-eyed. He stands alone. His great enterprise is all his own. His original shop at Muskoka Wharf is vastly enlarged. He has built a subsidiary plant at Orillia so that his larger vessels such as the hundred foot cruisers can have access to the sea via the Trent Canal. He will do this coming year $300,000 business, one cruiser alone to cost $60,000."

The *Star Weekly* story ended, "It is a story of success from the start, and so much of the success consists of something born in the blood and the breed, something instinctive and unteachable, like the ability to sing supremely—the gift of making planks and metal blossom into ships."

DITCHBURN

70' x 14' Cruiser built for John C. Hageman of New York, for use on Long Island Sound.

CUSTOM BUILT BOATS

Ditchburn Boats Catalogue

Left and following pages: In the late 1920s the Ditchburn Boat Company published a delightful catalogue as a review of their outstanding production success. Thirty-two vessels are pictured along with their owner's names. These elite customers comprised a veritable who's who of the yachting world in Canada and the United States.

The vessels include *Gannet*, a 100-foot yacht built for Commander J. K. L. Ross of Montreal; Mrs. Delphine Dodge Cromwell's 85-foot houseboat; *Yolanda*, a 65-foot schooner sailed by Commodore Norman Gooderham of Toronto; the famous Eaton boats *Kawandag II* and *Dolly Durkin*; the racing *Rainbows* of Harry Greening, plus many other fine yachts.

Very few boat builders in Canada or United States could have boasted of such an impressive fleet and their distinguished owners. We are fortunate to have been able to reproduce this brochure so that the extent of the Ditchburn production and the quality of their design and construction can be appreciated. To our knowledge only two of these vessels exist today. *Blythewood III* and *Rainbow III* are believed to be the only survivors.

Several later cruisers exist—the 1929 *High Tea*, the 1931 *Grace Anne II*, the 1935 *Birchbark* (now *Windswept III*) and the 1937 *Duchess*.

73' x 15' Day Express Cruiser built for Lady Eaton of Toronto, used at her Muskoka summer home.

Walter Cole's Fast Runabout Ben-Hur powered with 290 h.p. Sterling motor.

62' x 12' Cruiser owned by Fred W. Haines, Detroit, and used on the Great Lakes.

Lady Eaton's Sedan Runabout "DOLLY DURKIN," 38' x 7'6" with 300 h.p. motor, making 35 miles per hour.

A Special Sedan Runabout built of East India Vermilion Wood for Mr. George McLaughlin of Oshawa. Ont.

62' x 12' Cruiser owned by Fred W. Haines, Detroit, and used on the Great Lakes.

Rainbow IV. Winner American Gold Cup Race 1924. Holder of World's record for 24 hr. run 1218 miles.

Mr. H. B. Greening's Rainbow III. Fastest boat in America Gold Cup Race 1923. Broke word's record for 24 hour run in year now called Palm Beach Days and winner of more races than any other boat in America.

66′ x 12′ Twin Screw Cruiser built for P. D. Saylors, New York, President of Canada Dry Ginger Ale Co.

65′ x 13′ Cruiser built for Mr. Harry Hatch of Toronto. Powered with two Sterling 250 h.p. motors this boat has a speed of 21 m.p.h.

56′ x 11′ Fast Day Cruiser, built for Mr. J. Shoonmaker, of Cobourg, Ont. This boat is powered with two 300 h.p. motors and makes 30 m.p.h. Has splendid seagoing qualities.

Dr. Geo. Cooper's 34′ x 9′ Cruiser a very successful standardized model.

Mr. J. H. Hewitson of Brampton, 42′ Cruiser used on Georgian Bay.

"Nayada" a Class R. Racer built for Royal Canadian Yacht Club Syndicate. Winner of George Cup and many other championship races.

Yacht "GANNET" ploughing through waters of the Atlantic.

Yacht "GANNET" built for Commander J. K. L. Ross, Montreal, 100′ x 19′ powered with two 150 h.p. Diesel engines.

Commodore Austin H. Perry's 78′ x 14′ Seagoing Yacht built for use on Eastern seaboard. Speed with two 150 h.p. Speedway motors 17 m.p.h.

"Canadian Customs Patrol Boat "BEHAVE," one of a fleet of six developed for duty on the rough waters of the Atlantic Coast. Armed with machine guns and with full load and equipment these boats travel at 35 m.p.h. with 300 h.p.

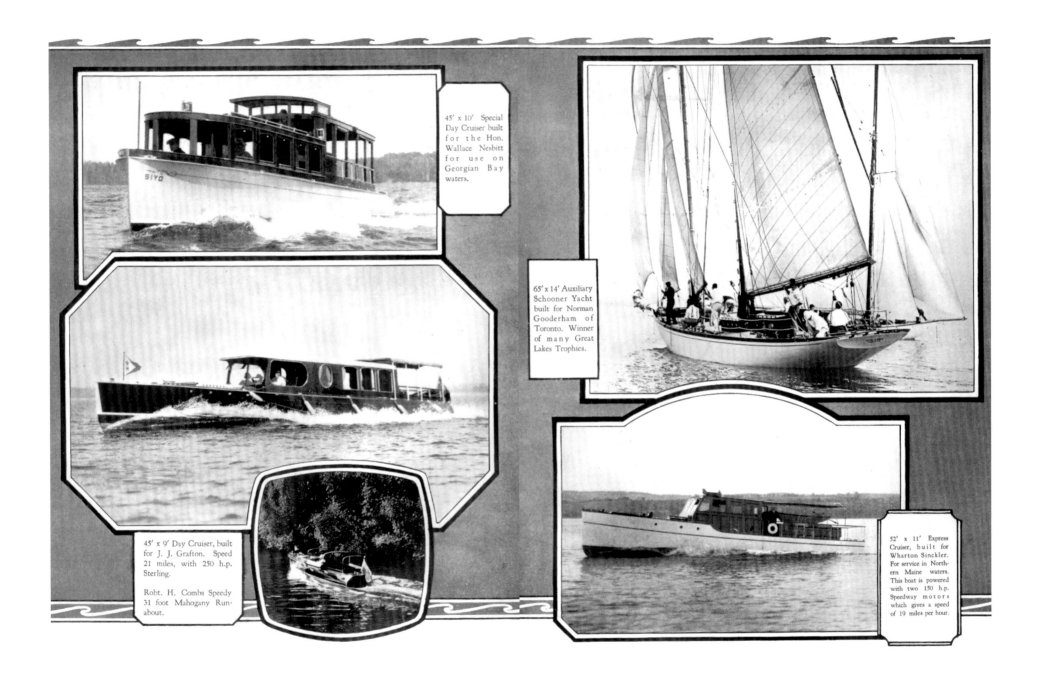

45' x 10' Special Day Cruiser built for the Hon. Wallace Nesbitt for use on Georgian Bay waters.

65' x 14' Auxiliary Schooner Yacht built for Norman Gooderham of Toronto. Winner of many Great Lakes Trophies.

45' x 9' Day Cruiser, built for J. J. Grafton. Speed 21 miles, with 250 h.p. Sterling.

Robt. H. Combs Speedy 31 foot Mahogany Runabout.

52' x 11' Express Cruiser, built for Wharton Sinckler. For service in Northern Maine waters. This boat is powered with two 150 h.p. Speedway motors which gives a speed of 19 miles per hour.

40' x 9' — Bridge deck "V" bottom Express Cruiser, built for Harry B. Greening.

Seeking the Haven of Happiness,
Where a Beacon of Welcome Gleams,
Down the Seas of the Centuries,
Man Sails the Ship of his Dreams.

This boat powered with 300 h.p. high speed light weight motor. Makes 32 m.p.h.

Rainbow II, a world record breaker photograph taken at 53 m.p.h.

Mr. H. A. Brown's 42' x 10'6' Cruiser powered with two 100 h.p. Kenneth motors.

45' x 10'6'' powered with 150 h.p. Sterling motor built for Mr. Lionel Smith of Montreal, Past Commodore of Royal St. Lawrence Yacht Club.

Rainbow I, owned by Sylvester Eagen of Buffalo. Twice winner of Fisher Gold Cup Race.

90' x 16' Houseboat, built for Mrs. Delphine Dodge Cromwell, New York. Speed 20 miles, with two 300 h.p. Wintons.

50' x 11' Cruiser built for Col. J. J. Blackstock, Toronto. At present in use on Lake Simcoe.

The Viking quickly became a very popular model, with its hard lines, its brawny, masculine, powerful hull shape, its raised engine hatch, elegant windscreen, and sparkling performance. New hardware, designed and manufactured by Ditchburn, graced the varnished decks. Leather seating for nine on three benches, plus the possibility of two more in wicker chairs, ensured that everybody could go along.

By 1927, the stepped-hull hydroplane was well known to the world, but the racing fraternity had first recognized its virtues. Ditchburn had by now much experience in racing, having built the famous *Rainbows*, raced by Harry Greening to capture world attention and Gold Cup honours for Canada. But now the desire for greater speed and the ego-driven need to own the fastest craft on the lake were influencing the family runabout market. Round-bilged displacement hulls had long dominated the protected waters of Muskoka, but now an exciting and different product came onto the market.

It had long been understood that the displacement hull, which cuts through the water, was subject to upper limits of speed. It can easily be driven to a speed equal to the square root of its waterline length, but then it gets a lot tougher. Added power increases wave-making, the stern is depressed, and a maximum speed is achieved in the order of 1.4 times the square root of the waterline length. More power will not increase the speed; to go faster the hull must be able to rise up in the water and hydroplane across its surface.

Pioneer British designer and builder S. E. (Sam) Saunders of Cowes, England, had built several stepped-hull vessels before the First World War, including the multi-stepped, 40-foot *Maple Leaf IV*, the first boat in the world to attain a speed of 50 knots. She defeated the American entries in 1912 and 1913 for the

Harmsworth Trophy, proving the efficiency of her hull design. It is interesting to compare her speed with present-day vessels of similar size and horsepower, for while these modern boats all have engines of less than one-quarter the weight per horsepower of *Maple Leaf IV*, very few go as fast. You'll find this by dividing the top speed in knots by the square root of the waterline length to produce a speed ratio. *Maple Leaf*'s top end of 55 knots is divided by the square root of the waterline length, 6.32184, to produce a speed ratio of 8.7.

Sam Saunders' success with stepped hulls would have been well known to the Ditchburn group, particularly to Bert Hawker, designer and plant foreman. An Englishman who had come to Canada in 1907, Hawker had found work with several Ontario boat builders, including Minett, and upon returning home from the war in 1919, had become an important member of the Ditchburn team. While the designer of the new Viking model is not mentioned in company literature, it was probably largely Hawker's work.

The sales brochure described the new Viking as a "standardized Gentleman's Runabout, the fastest boat of its class ever built," and further claimed "unusual speed of 40 to 45 mph with a 150 horsepower engine, made possible by the scientific application of under body lines which greatly eliminate resistance caused by vacuum and wetted surface."

One picture illustrates the vessel carrying eleven passengers, a load of 1,700 pounds, and still being able to achieve a speed of 36 mph. A reference is also made to the Ditchburn-built *Rainbow I*, Harry Greening's winner of the Fisher Trophy Race in Miami in 1920 and 1921. "The Viking is 5 and ½ miles faster per hour with a 150 hp motor than the *Rainbow I* which carried a 300 hp motor."

Ditchburn credited their experience in producing six high-speed patrol boats for the Canadian government as the inspiration for the design. These 38-footers, with Lewis machine guns mounted on the foredeck, were kept busy on the Atlantic coast chasing down rum-runners. Ditchburn had won the contract by guaranteeing

Above: A more conventional forward-drive version of the Viking hull was also built.

Opposite above: Mowitza II, the first of the new 27-foot Vikings was illustrated in the brochure carrying eleven passengers.

Opposite below: Phyllis, another 1928 Viking, shows her clean planing form.

Above: A useful brochure described the new Viking in detail.

Opposite: Hibiscus, a 1929 model, demonstrates the agile performance and sea-keeping qualities of the Viking stepped hull. Owned by the Hermann family, this vessel is in excellent condition. Her original engine, a Kermath, still powers the vessel.

a speed of 31 mph for these fast and seaworthy revenue cutters. They could actually achieve 35 mph, fully loaded and manned by a crew of three, and the government promptly ordered five more.

It is probable the speed claims of the Viking brochure were somewhat overstated, but with the larger Sterling and Kermath engines introduced the following year, the Vikings could indeed surpass the 40-mph mark. Several of the surviving 27 foot Vikings have been repowered with V-8 engines for even livelier performance, but the significant weight reduction may cause trim problems.

A single-stepped hydroplane is designed to ride on two points of the hull—amidships, just ahead of the step, and on the hull bottom right aft. Its advantage over a non-stepped hull is that it just rises bodily out of the water, fore and aft the same amount, and skims along the top. The angle of attack is built into her, so she does not have to alter her trim in order to plane, as does a stepless boat.

Speed claims aside, the Viking quickly became a very popular model, with its hard lines,

its brawny, masculine, powerful hull shape, its raised engine hatch, elegant windscreen, and sparkling performance. New hardware, designed and manufactured by Ditchburn, graced the varnished decks. Leather seating for nine on three benches, plus the possibility of two more in wicker chairs, ensured that everybody could go along.

The principal measurements of this boat are a 27-foot length, with a beam of 6 feet, 6 inches, a draft of 2 feet, and a weight of around 5,000 pounds, depending on engine choice. The keel and framework are of selected, air-dried white oak. Planking above the waterline is African or Mexican mahogany, figured stock. Planking below is clear, selected cedar or cypress. Fastenings to frames are copper rivets with heads countersunk and plugged to match planking. Decks are African or Mexican mahogany, edge nailed and blind fastened to white oak carlins, and seams are caulked and payed with bright yellow compound.

Forward of the engine compartment is a waterproof, cedar bulkhead with a fireproofing

material on the engine side. Aft of the engine is another waterproofed, soundproofed, and fire-proofed bulkhead, with mahogany on the passenger side. The cockpit floor is made of removable mahogany gratings, while the engine-room flooring is plywood covered in aluminum corrugated matting. The driver's bench has a removable centre section to allow access to the rear; the stern seat back is removable to allow access to the steering gear and main gasoline tank. An auxiliary fuel tank is fitted in the forward compartment.

Four instruments are mounted in an AC German silver panel, itself mounted on a varnished walnut panel fastened to the mahogany bulkhead. The lower section of the windscreen is mahogany-framed plate glass, with two adjustable and unbreakable, hinged-

The quality of Ditchburn construction is evident on *Mowitza II*.

Modern Craft With Modern Power

MOWITZA II, *owned by Mr. F. Burgess of Toronto, built by Ditchburn and powered by Sterling. Speed 42 M. P. H.*

glass plates attached to its upper edge for added wind protection.

Exposed wood was covered with six coats of spar varnish and four coats on protected surfaces. The hull below the water got two coats of lead-based paints and two coats of marine bottom paint. Above the water, the hull was finished natural with five coats of varnish. All the materials used were of the best grade and highest quality, and the engineering and workmanship was of the highest standard.

Still, it was not a boat for everyone. An elderly Muskoka cottager recalled Tom Greavette, then sales manager for Ditchburn, coming to the

Above: The fully loaded *Mowitza II* demonstrates her speed in a company advertisement of the time.

103

family island to demonstrate the new vessel to his father. Apparently it was not a good day for the demonstration, as a light breeze grew steadily stronger, and the long uphill pounding to home dock convinced the family to order a more conventional Minett-Shields launch, which offered a slower but more familiar ride.

Probably the best known of the seven known survivors is *Mowitza II*, ordered in September 1928 by Fred Burgess, an experienced and devoted boater who had visited the Toronto showroom on King Street to finalize his purchase. Delivered in June of 1929, *Mowitza II* was immediately put to the test in the Muskoka Lakes Association Annual Regatta, where she scored a second in the senior motorboat event. In 1930, she won her class when *Whippet*, an out-and-out race boat, broke an oil line. She also competed well for another three years, but the exact rankings remain unknown.

To prepare for these important competitions, the vessel had been lifted at the Gravenhurst factory, allowed to dry out for several hours, then had her bottom polished with a graphite

Opposite: The 1929 *Voodoo*, owned by Anthony Miller of Toronto, is still powered by her original Sterling engine.

Above: A cartoon in *Canadian Power Boating* of February 1930 profiled Herb Ditchburn, noting his "hard work and inherent ability" as a boat builder.

compound. She was then fuelled with only 15 gallons of gasoline to keep her weight down. On occasion, ether, oil, and airplane gas were added to the tank as secret ingredients.

Despite her racing success that first summer, her new owner had some complaints that he took back to Herb Ditchburn. While Ditchburn work was always to the highest standards, Fred Burgess felt the foredeck planking was not matched and varnished to his satisfaction. In addition, he had now seen *Mint Julep*, a Viking recently delivered to the Eaton family, and the latter vessel had a more elegant dashboard and instrument panel than the one fitted in *Mowitza*. Two small shelves port and starboard had also been added to this area.

Herb Ditchburn wrote to Burgess on July 2, 1929, to confirm that the company would respond immediately to all these concerns: "We appreciate that your boat is being used alongside some of our competitor's best," he stated in his letter, "and are therefore anxious to bring it into a condition which will leave no room for criticism." Don't you wish you could

get a warranty response like that today! But this was not an isolated incident. Ditchburn quality was always high, and Herb Ditchburn never hesitated to keep it that way.

Burgess paid $5,870.50 for his *Viking*, which was a fair price for a top, new, custom product from Canada's largest builder of high-quality yachts. It was far beyond the workingman's range, but wealthy Muskoka residents were enthusiastic, and twenty hulls were sold in the next two years. Unfortunately, the disastrous stock-market crash was just around the corner, and luxury boat builders were to suffer the most.

Today we can enjoy seven survivors of the original twenty *Vikings* produced—six in Ontario and one at Lake Tahoe in California. Their daring design, flashy performance, and handsome appearance never fail to attract attention. They remain a signature work that would never have come from an ordinary builder.

Opposite: **The 1930 *Ponder* shows some acceleration with owner Tom Ballantyne at the helm. This vessel has been repowered with a 454-cubic-inch V-8 engine.**

The Patent Story

A totally unknown story came to light in researching Herb Ditchburn's personal records. Always wanting to be on the leading edge of technical development, Ditchburn and a friend, an engineer named Charles Shaw, had secretly been researching and developing a hydrofoil to be mounted under the hull of the 27-foot Viking to enhance its already remarkable speed and to lessen the power requirement to attain that speed.

Cast in aluminum, this V-shaped foil was to be mounted just forward of the midship step and would provide lift as speed increased. Eventually, the dead weight of the hull and its wetted surface would be significantly reduced, while smoother, safer riding and turning would be accomplished, according to Shaw and Ditchburn.

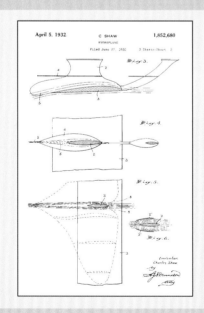

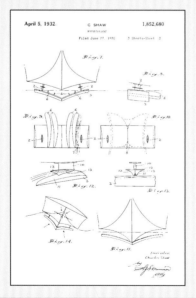

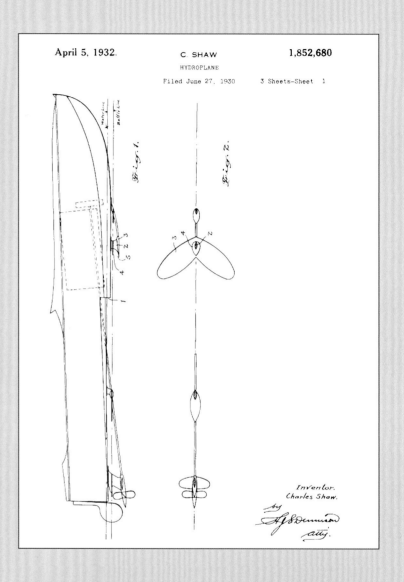

Above and left: Several illustrations from the 1930 hydroplane patent. Ditchburn and Shaw had spent many months calculating lifting forces, stability, and other engineering considerations.

Left: A specially built vessel is tested with the Ditchburn stern gear and outdrive.

Below: An article in *Canadian Power Boating* of January 1930 commented on Herb Ditchburn's invention.

New Power and Steering Unit

Interesting New Device Being Developed in Ditchburn Shops

THE writer has had the opportunity to follow the experimental work that has been underway in the Ditchburn, Gravenhurst, shops relating to the Stern Gear Drive which has been the ambition of many to perfect.

In the Ditchburn Stern Gear Drive the power is taken direct from the engine clutch—no reverse gear is necessary—and applied through bevel gears to the vertical shaft; another set of bevel gears transmit power to the propeller. With the exception of the upper bevel gears the unit is much the same as the practice in outboard motor design.

There are two main objections to this form of drive. First, the loss of power through the gears. Secondly, the engine weight being so far aft. The loss of engine power would not exceed ten percent which is more than overcome by the gain in efficiency obtainable through arranging correct gear ratios between engine and propeller and because of the zero-angle of the propeller to the advance of the boat.

Secondly the weight being aft can be supported by giving greater beam and buoyancy where it is needed. In the accompanying photo the effect of this heavy weight aft can be discerned in the bad angle at which the boat is running. This boat was not designed for this rear gear drive and was only fitted with same for experimental purposes. The plan reproduced herewith shows a 24 footer designed especially for this form of drive.

Another difficulty that all previous experimenters have discovered is that of the tendency of the power egg to revolve around the vertical shaft. It is understood Mr. Ditchburn has overcome this problem.

After having explained the drawbacks to this form of drive,

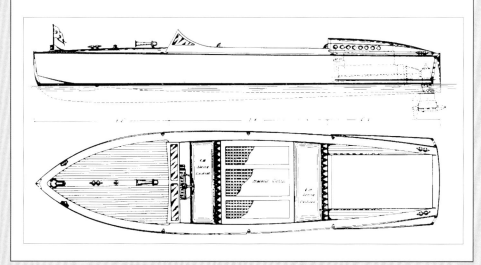

Unfortunately, it appears that their theories were never put to the test. Ditchburn had agreed to pay the cost of the patent attorney, but he was overcome by business problems threatening the future of the company. The United States Patent Office issued patent number 1,852,680, dated April 5, 1932, in the name of Charles Shaw alone. There is no record or knowledge of any attempt to test the invention.

Shaw and Ditchburn had also cooperated on the development of a stern drive, for which the United States Patent Office issued patent number 1,765,789 on June 24, 1930, to Herbert Ditchburn, of Gravenhurst, Ontario, Canada.

At the time, at least a dozen American companies were marketing a stern drive or a V-drive, all trying to solve the same problems—more passenger room in the boat, less noise and exhaust fumes, and easier installation of a standard propulsion unit. These companies included Outboard Marine Corp., Gray Marine Motor Co., Columbian Bronze Co., Capitol Gear, D. W. Onan and Sons, and many others. None worked well enough to achieve marketing success, and many years passed before the outdrive became practical and widely used.

Ditchburn's design involved a tractor propeller, which could be operated in either direction, and a rudder, which could be operated independently. At least one unit was built and tested on a specially built hull, but the story seems to end there. Overcome by the pressing financial problems that enveloped the company, all experimentation ceased.

Undoubtedly every Ditchburn boat could tell a story if indeed they could talk, and since we can't tell them all it's perhaps unfair to tell any. But some are so unusual, so charming, so unbelievable, that they just have to be told!

GRACE ANNE II

The last major vessel to be launched at Orillia was an 85-foot, houseboat-styled cruiser commissioned by John Forlong of Kenora, a colourful entrepreneur who wanted a new and larger vessel to be used on Lake of the Woods, as a surprise birthday present for his wife.

Around 1913, John Forlong had won a 52-foot cruiser in a high-stakes poker game, named it *Grace Anne* in honour of his wife, and for eighteen years used it to explore the wilderness areas of that huge water. John's father-in-law, Alexander MacDonald, had established a summer home on nearby Coney Island, and on his death this property was inherited by the Forlongs. The combination of cottage home and lake exploration by yacht was exactly to their liking, and summer weekends were filled with family and friends.

Knowing of the Ditchburn reputation for style, workmanship, and engineering excellence, Forlong chose this builder to carry out the next project he had envisioned. *Grace Anne II* was to be 85 feet in length by 17 feet in beam,

Grace Anne and John Forlong, owners of *Grace Anne II*.

with a draught of 5 feet. Her gross tonnage would be 105.63 tons, and powered by a single, 300-horsepower Sterling engine, she was expected to cruise at 12 knots. But her home was to be on Lake of the Woods, which is not connected to the Great Lakes. Thus her complicated rail delivery to those waters had to be ensured before production could begin.

Months of precision planning between the Ditchburn Company and Canadian National Railway officials of the Port Arthur division were required. Minimum clearances at rock cuts, bridges, water tanks, and coaling stations had to be checked. Superelevation of curves was considered, to determine whether the load might be thrown off centre and overturned. Eventually, as a final check, a scale model was built and tested on a small-scale track to determine that all information was correct.

Naturally, for transport, the completed vessel would have to be stripped of her deckhouse and all external fittings. Her 17-foot beam exceeded several bridge spans, so it would be necessary for the hull to travel on its side, and a special cradle would be required to hold the hull in its travel position. Finally, it was all agreed to be possible, and construction began.

After four months and at an estimated cost of $75,000, the *Grace Anne II* was ready for launching. With flags flying, the town band playing, and Herbert's daughter, Josephine Ditchburn, breaking the customary champagne bottle on her bow, she slid into the water to the cheers of workers and guests.

Unfortunately, this triumphant day was almost coincident with the demise of the Ditchburn Boat Building Co. With the Depression that had followed the stock-market crash, orders had disappeared, two thirds of the workforce had been laid off, and the last two orders to be filled at the Orillia plant were a 117-foot patrol boat for the federal government and the houseboat cruiser *Grace Anne II*.

Now, Captain Arthur Davies was ready to undertake the long and complicated journey from Orillia through the Trent-Severn Canal to Georgian Bay, Lakes Huron and Superior to Port Arthur—a 1,285-mile trip. This phase was accomplished with a minimum of difficulty, the vessel behaving as expected. The second phase, from Port Arthur to Rainy River at the southeast end of the Lake of the Woods, had to be made by rail. It was a monumental feat, never before attempted with such a large vessel.

When the boat arrived in Port Arthur, the Port Arthur Shipbuilding Co. took eleven days to remove the deckhouse and all external fittings. The hull was then lifted on its side into the

Very exacting arrangements were needed to transport the 85-foot houseboat to her home on Lake of the Woods.

Above: The bridge and instrumentation of *Grace Anne II* have been continually updated.

Right: Ditchburn quality is still breathtaking.

Opposite: Always faultlessly maintained by her various owners, this stately houseboat still looks very much as it did originally. Photo courtesy Salisbury Cruises Ltd., Kenora, Ontario.

large, special cradle designed for her rail transport. The cradled, 85-foot hull was then lifted onto a 61-foot flatcar, and her engine, deckhouse and all other parts were loaded onto three additional flatcars. Herb Ditchburn himself had come to Port Arthur to work with railroad officials in completing this most difficult shipment.

Despite an overhead bridge clearance near Fort Frances of only 2 inches, *Grace Anne II* arrived in Rainy River without a single crack in her painted finish—a testimonial to careful handling and exacting planning. There on the banks of the river, the houseboat was reassembled, launched, and piloted to her new home at Kenora, on the north side of the lake. Arriving on August 12, she was immediately installed in her new boathouse, where the six men who had accompanied her put the finishing touches to her hull and machinery. In September, she took her first official run, to Crow Rock and back.

Enjoying a cruise on the *Grace Anne II* would be an easy assignment.

No expense was spared in furnishing this luxurious yacht to make it the finest on the lake. The Forlongs entertained lavishly on afternoon and overnight cruises, each trip allowing the family and their guests to enjoy the incredible scenery, fishing without equal, and wilderness exploration in spacious, self-sufficient comfort. *Grace Anne II* carried 1,000 gallons of fresh water, 1,000 gallons of gasoline, and had a cruising range of 1,000 miles.

In 1946, the boat was sold to Ralph Erwin, who ran it as a cruise and charter ship for his Salisbury House restaurant chain. Charter price for the six-day cruise, accommodating twelve to fifteen guests, was $2,500. For a limited time, daily cruises were offered as well. Guests paid $10 for the daylong cruise, with lunch and dinner included.

By 1950, the *Grace Anne II* was being operated as a private club with seven shareholders, each entitled to three weeks cruising time. A share cost $6,000 plus a $2,000 annual fee for maintenance and operation. The 3M company of St. Paul bought into this venture, eventually purchasing all remaining shares in 1954. For the next forty years the vessel served the needs of a growing number of 3M service and product divisions.

During the 3M ownership, vast sums of money were spent to preserve and maintain the *Grace Anne II*, always with the objective of retaining the original character of the vessel and the high quality of its Ditchburn craftsmanship. Throughout all the years of their ownership, the vessel lost none of its unique style, its superb craftsmanship, or its Ditchburn distinction.

In 1994, the vessel's captain, along with several other former employees, purchased the beautifully preserved cruiser from 3M, forming a new company, Salisbury Cruises, to charter the vessel for wedding parties, company meetings, family getaways, fishing friends, and other unforgettable cruising experiences. Threading her way through the thousands of pine covered islands on one of the most beautiful lakes in the world, the seventy-year-old *Grace Anne II*, the largest Ditchburn yacht still afloat, continues to provide a wilderness experience in pampered luxury.

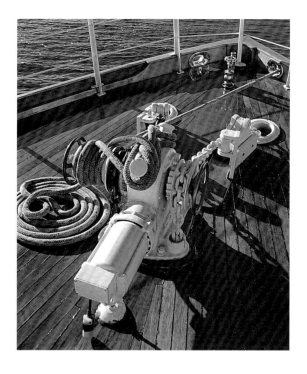

The power windlass on the foredeck makes anchoring a pleasure.

Eccentric Marion "Joe" Carstairs drove everything from ambulances to motorcars, from schooners to hydroplanes, always at full throttle. Assisted by her mechanic, Joe Harris, she became the fastest woman on the water, and a Ditchburn customer. Photo by Lambert of Getty Images.

ESTELLE V

One of the most bizarre episodes in Ditchburn history centres on the race boat *Estelle V*, a 35-foot hydroplane powered by two 900-horsepower Napier Lion engines, designed by Bert Hawker, built in England, but completed, tested, and perfected at Ditchburn's in Muskoka. The owner was a most unusual woman, Marion Barbara Carstairs, who preferred to be known as "Joe."

A flamboyant character, mannish in appearance and dress, given to smoking cigars, sporting tattoos, and always seeking adventures not ordinarily available to young women, English-born Miss Carstairs was fabulously wealthy, her American grandfather being one of the founders of Standard Oil. Her beautiful mother married many times, travelled the world, and generally ignored Marion. Throughout the First World War, Marion drove ambulances in France, seeking out dangerous living. Then in the 1920s she turned to boats and the world of speed.

In 1927, Carstairs commissioned three hydroplanes to be built in secrecy, hoping to

break the 100-mile-per-hour mark. Named *Estelle I, II,* and *III,* these vessels did not accomplish her goal but did make her the fastest woman on the water. In September 1928, she was a challenger in the tiny, 21-foot *Estelle II* for the Harmsworth Trophy at Detroit, where Gar Wood's *Miss America VII* dwarfed her. The British challenger actually led for a half lap, but broached, nose-dived and sank, succumbing to a tremendous stern wave from her larger rival.

Gamely, she returned the next year with *Estelle IV,* a much larger vessel, at 35 feet by 9.5 feet, which had been brought to Muskoka for summer testing in advance of the September racing. Powered by three Napier engines, the

Above: In her first Harmsworth challenge in 1928, Carstairs and *Estelle II* experienced an unexpected sinking.

Below: Estelle V didn't win, but for the first time Gar Wood's *Miss Americas* were seriously challenged.

race boat handled badly, especially on turns. Bert Hawker and Herb Ditchburn finally decided to remove the third engine, and while handling was improved, the loss of top speed made her an easy victim for Gar Wood's new *Miss America VIII*.

Carstairs had turned to Bert Hawker as designer for *Estelle IV*, and now again for *Estelle V*, as she had recognized his skill and daring. By the Harmsworth rules the vessel had

to be built in the challenging country, which was done, but then it was shipped to Lake Muskoka for rigorous shakedown and fine-tuning. The new *Estelle V* was very fast, a much better performer, and both Ditchburn and Hawker began to express some confidence. Rumours had the new boat clocked at 94 mph. Meanwhile, Joe Carstairs was now living in rental quarters in Muskoka, shocking the natives, but preparing herself for the big test at Detroit.

On August 30, five unlimited racers came to the start line—*Estelle IV* and *Estelle V*, with Joe Carstairs driving the older vessel, and three *Miss Americas*—*IX*, *VIII*, and *V*—driven by three Wood brothers, Gar, George, and Phil. The winner was only briefly in doubt, but it still provided the first real challenge to Gar Wood's domination of the Harmsworth Trophy.

In the first 30-mile heat, *Estelle IV* was first

Hawker's design for *Estelle V* is revealed in this drawing of her internal layout. Enclosed shafts from the two Napier engines are carried forward to V-drives, then through secondary shafts to the propellers.

across the start line with three American boats in hot pursuit. By the end of the first lap, the two newest U.S. racers had passed Carstairs and enjoyed an enormous lead. But now the danger-loving Hawker seemed to come from nowhere, relentlessly cutting down the distance to the leaders.

Both of the American boats were running faster now—they had to—*Estelle V* was visibly gaining on them. A press plane flying overhead filmed the dramatic moment as Hawker surged into the lead, but then disaster struck. Hardly had the *Estelle V* taken the lead when her gas tank split and an oil line broke. Hawker, his goggles covered in oil, was blinded, and travelling at more than 90 mph. Veering off the course, the 8,000-pound challenger shot dangerously across George Wood's course, and then threaded, fate-guided, through a dozen spectator craft, before the mechanic could shut her down.

Unaware of the disaster and stung by *Estelle V*'s speed, the American boats pounded downstream towards the finish of the second lap. Hawker lost no time in getting underway

Estelle IV was larger but slower than *Estelle V*.

again, and although gasoline was flowing around the cockpit and oil was escaping from one engine, the chase was on. Even with all the lost time, *Estelle V* was within 200 yards of the leaders as they passed the judges' stand.

Of course, the chase could not last for long. A quarter mile past the start line, the last of the gasoline leaked away and *Estelle V* was dead in the water. By requiring a tow from the course she was disqualified from competition.

On Monday, September 1, the second heat got underway with only *Estelle IV* to carry the British hopes. Joe Carstairs graciously

surrendered her seat to Bert Hawker as the better driver, but even though he was able to produce a little more speed, the issue was never in doubt. With no chance of losing, Gar Wood drove his newest defender to a heat record of 77.39 mph. In the years following 1920, when Wood first captured the trophy at Osborne Bay, England, he had edged the winning speed up a small margin at each defence, from 61.51 mph to 77.39 mph in 1930.

Marion "Joe" Carstairs now abandoned the racing scene, but then began an even more bizarre chapter of her life by purchasing a wild, sparsely populated island in the Bahamas for $40,000. Here she built a residence, roads, and a yacht harbour, organized an "army," and entertained the Duke and Duchess of Windsor. British author Kate Summerscale recently documented her eccentric life in *The Queen of Whale Cay*.

Herb Ditchburn and Bert Hawker could probably have written an entertaining volume of their own experiences with the fastest woman on the water.

Above: *Whisper*, the union picket boat, bears down on a strikebreaker.

Below: The cover of the union publication honours the role played by *Whisper*.

WHISPER, THE UNION BOAT

A 31-foot Ditchburn launch that left the Gravenhurst factory in 1929 has recently returned to Lake Muskoka after an exacting restoration. If this vessel could talk, she would have some tall tales to tell, as her various careers have included chauffeur-driven cottage service, rum-running, picket duty for a striking union, hotel livery duty, and the transportation of several private owners.

Sold by her first owner, the sleek mahogany *Whisper*, hull number 29-14, was delivered to a Hamilton operator for use on Lake Erie, where her low profile and high speed were put to immediate use delivering special cargo to the Cleveland area. Little is officially recorded of these nighttime voyages, but her owner apparently went out of business with the 1934 repeal of U.S. prohibition.

Her next owner was also in the bootlegging business but confined his deliveries to various lakeshore dance palaces in the Hamilton, Burlington, Bronte, and Oakville areas. Always a speedy vessel, she had a Kermath Sea Wolf engine refitted with new Zenith carburetors, which took her top speed to over 40 mph, allowing her to run away from most other lake traffic.

In 1946, she experienced a most amazing career change. Purchased by Local 1005 of the United Steel Workers of America, *Whisper* was taken to Hamilton Harbour to play a unique role in a bitter labour dispute. In newspaper accounts of the time, *Whisper* figured regularly as the strikers struggled to prevent water access to the strike-bound plant, while management endeavoured to maintain production and supply food to non-striking workers in the mill. Any boats approaching the area were subjected to threats, harassment, and swamping by the patrolling picket boat. Shots were fired on one occasion, ending in arrests by the Hamilton Harbour police with resulting fines and jail sentences. After the long dispute was settled, the union commissioned the publication of a book entitled *It Started with a Whisper*, a history of the 1946 strike and the important role played by its Ditchburn launch.

Complete restoration of *Whisper* begins seventy years later.

To recoup its investment, the union raffled off the vessel, and a Hamilton fuel-oil dealer became the lucky winner of the now-famous launch. A later owner sold her to the newly opened Muskoka Sands resort hotel, where she transported guests for many years. In 1993, she was sold to a Michigan boater who intended to completely restore the aging craft, but that never happened, as other projects commanded the owner's attention.

Recently, Collingwood and Lake Muskoka resident Duncan Hawkins, an antique-boat enthusiast and past president of the Antique and Classic Boat Society of Toronto, learned of *Whisper*, then languishing in a Michigan storage shed. Hawkins, who had worked his student summers at the steel mill, knew something of *Whisper's* unique history and quickly decided that this proud Ditchburn launch should be restored and returned to her home waters in Muskoka.

Hawkins vowed that this would be an authentic restoration, taking *Whisper* back to her original equipment and appearance. A restored

Far left: A keyless, rim-wind clock was one of a hundred original items of hardware.

Left: A powerful horn graces the foredeck.

Opposite: The impressive size and speed of *Whisper* were used to enforce the picket line.

Kermath Sea Wolf was located in Minnesota and over one hundred pieces of correct and authentic Ditchburn hardware found, including a keyless, rim-wind, eight-day clock for mounting on the dash. Eighty percent of her original planking could be used, but a new keel and some replacement ribs were needed.

The replacement of her original one-piece transom was somewhat more difficult, but eventually the right plank of solid mahogany was found, soaked for two months, then bent into position using steam. Finally, in August 2001, *Whisper* was back in her home waters of Lake Muskoka, throwing a powerful wake as she cruised easily at 35 mph—that same wake that must have terrified the small craft at the steel-plant strike.

Hawkins made an enormous investment to return this vessel to top condition, but knowing her history, having worked in the mill during student summers, it seemed to become an obligation. Or perhaps an obsession.

Says Hawkins, "There seems to be a certain sense of stewardship involved. Most of the old union crew are now gone, but I would still like to take *Whisper* to Hamilton Harbour some day. And maybe we'd need some volunteer scabs in tin boats to swamp."

In retrospect, it is easy to mark the warning signs, but to Herb Ditchburn, who had never known anything but growth and success, it was difficult to foresee that the economic depression now underway was to last throughout the 1930s.

In August of 1930, Tom Greavette resigned from the company. This was a terrible blow to Ditchburn Boats, as Tom had been employed there pretty well all his life. He had started as a youth, learned the boat-building trade, become a director when the company had been incorporated in 1907, and for many years had been their chief salesman. But times had changed dramatically. The stock market crash in late 1929 had almost immediately ended the market for custom watercraft and luxury goods of all kinds.

Greavette envisioned a new kind of boat building—production-line methods of smaller craft that would bring a lower-cost product to the customer. He was supported in this vision by his financial backers, most of whom were past customers, owners of Ditchburn boats. His directors had even suggested that the new company be named "Rainbow Boats," in a clumsy attempt to capitalize on Greening's racing success. This provoked a predictable response from Herb Ditchburn, whose company had been totally identified with Greening's *Rainbows*, and the idea was quickly dropped.

In fact, Tom Greavette was wrong, or at least ahead of his time. After several years of producing the Dart boat under licence from the Toledo, Ohio, builder, it became obvious that what market existed in Muskoka was for limited numbers of custom or semi-custom boats. The newly formed Greavette Boat Works never achieved the envisioned production-line method of manufacture.

The swift collapse of orders for large and small boats was an immediate concern for Ditchburn, and by July of 1930 it became necessary to lay off workers. By 1931, the situation was desperate, with two thirds of the workforce laid off. The only significant work for the winter of 1931 was at the Orillia factory—the 85-foot houseboat for the Lake of the Woods, and a 117-foot patrol boat for the federal government, which was likely to be a money loser, taken on in desperation.

In retrospect, it is easy to mark the warning signs, but to Herb Ditchburn, who had never known anything but growth and success, it was difficult to foresee that the economic depression now underway was to last throughout the 1930s. In thirty years, the company had progressed from simple rowing boats to sophisticated 100-foot yachts, from a small local industry to Canada's most significant boat builder, from a handful of workmen to a major employer in both Gravenhurst and Orillia.

In 1929, the Gravenhurst plant had been doubled in size, and the *Orillia Packet and Times* reported on November 21 that "the prospect for the future of the Orillia plant is most encouraging." This was one month after the October crash, but few people in Muskoka were important traders on the New York Stock Exchange. The stunning reversal of fortune was hard to accept, and no one anticipated that the entire 1930s would be a depressed decade.

Past success and growth undoubtedly clouded management's vision of the future, and expansion of facilities had placed a financial burden on the company. Reluctance to lay off workers, who were all personal friends, knowing that alternative employment did not exist, delayed management's action. The failure to diversify into other products less susceptible to market downturns, and the dependence on wealthy customers were also factors that played a role. But the most damaged by these unbelievable changes was undoubtedly the man at the helm. Herb Ditchburn, who had failed to secure his own financial position by selling stock in his company, lost his home, his company, his self-respect, and some friends. It was a crushing blow for a self-made man.

After a decade of growth, Ditchburn Boats Ltd. had no orders for new craft, and on May 26, 1932, the proud company was declared bankrupt. The suddenness and the extent of the market crash can hardly be imagined today, but it has been calculated that between October 1929 and January 1932, the New York market lost 81 percent of its value.

A year later, it was reorganized as the Ditchburn Boat and Yachting Co., and a line of smaller boats, from 18 to 24 feet, was introduced—more realistic for the reduced market. These modest craft were still built to Ditchburn standards of quality construction

The Bankruptcy Act

IN THE ESTATE OF DITCHBURN BOATS, LIMITED, of Gravenhurst Ontario, BANKRUPT.

NOTICE IS HEREBY GIVEN that Ditchburn Boats Limited of Gravenhurst, Ontario, was adjudged bankrupt and a Receiving Order made on the 26th day of May, 1932, and that William J. Reilly, Registrar, has appointed me to be Custodian of the estate of the debtor until the first meeting of the Creditors.

NOTICE IS FURTHER GIVEN that the first meeting of Creditors in the above estate will be held at the office of the Official Receiver at Osgoode Hall, Toronto, on the 16th day of June, 1932, at 2.30 o'clock in the afternoon (Daylight Saving Time).

To entitle you to vote thereat, proof of your claim must be lodged with me before the meeting is held. Proxies to be used at the meeting must be lodged with me prior thereto.

And further take notice that at such meeting the Creditors will elect the permanent Trustee.

AND FURTHER TAKE NOTICE that if you have any claim against the debtor for which you are entitled to rank, proof of such claim must be filed with me, or with the Trustee when appointed, within thirty days from the date of this notice, otherwise the proceeds of the debtor's estate will be distributed among the parties entitled thereto without regard to your claim.

DATED at Toronto this 2nd day of June, 1932.

G. T. CLARKSON, Custodian,
Co. E. R. Clarkson & Sons,
15 Wellington St. West,
23a   Toronto 2, Ontario.

Despite thirty years of growth and development the Depression found another victim.

but lacked the luxury details of previous models. But the Depression market was spotty at best, and the company soon failed again.

Reorganized one last time in 1936 as Ditchburn Boat and Aircraft Ltd., the company now had shareholders who envisioned wider markets and an expanded range of products. Airplane construction under licence was investigated but never undertaken. Several larger vessels were built, including *Birch Bark*, a 52-foot cruiser delivered to Georgian Bay, and *Duchess*, a 40-foot cruiser delivered to Montreal. Three 64-foot hulls were built for the Royal Canadian Mounted Police, apparently at a small loss. In all, company records show that while 44 vessels were completed in 1937, an operating loss of $1637.10 resulted.

Advertisements published during the 1930s emphasized value and practicality. Quality was maintained but simpler, less expensive vessels were featured.

130

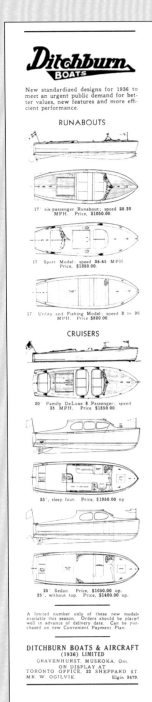
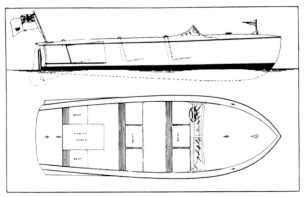

The company had been profitable from its incorporation in 1907 until 1929, the last year having been its greatest period of both sales and profit. In 1930 and 1931, sales slipped to 79 percent and 55 percent of the 1929 record, but profits disappeared entirely. The short-lived second incorporation never achieved profits, operating as it did in the depths of the Depression, and with no working capital. The third company had not made any profit, but sales volume was growing. If they could have survived another year or two, the war work that arrived for all boat builders would probably have saved the day.

Time ran out in March 1938, when the final incorporation was forced to declare bankruptcy. It was the sad end to a glorious chapter in Canadian boat building.

Above: The 1933 *Evangeline*, a 20-foot utility model, has seen seventy years of service.

Left: Launched as *Birch Bark* in 1935, this handsome 52-foot cruiser first sailed in Georgian Bay. Later, in Muskoka, she was christened *Jogwendi*. Now at harbour in Toronto, she is owned by Gordon Russell and named *Windswept III*.
Photo courtesy Gordon Russell.

Below and right: The white-hulled, 25-foot, 4-inch *Kemah II* dates to 1934. With a semi-displacement hull, she is not typical of Ditchburn production of the period, being much more elegant and built to the highest standards of custom work. Designed by Earle Barnes, *Kemah II* exhibits many details of his style, such as the three-piece raked-back windscreen, the moulding treatment around the "mother-in-law" seat, the wider beam, and the sloping rear deck. Restored in 1994, *Kemah II* proceeded to win many show awards including Boat of the Year at Gravenhurst, Best in Show at Lake Tahoe, Best Launch at Clayton and Captain's Choice at Manotick.

Below and right: Glenelda II was built as a 37-foot cruiser and launched in 1935. Her lines reflect the art deco style of those times. (Remember the Chrysler Airflo and Streamliner trains?) Her present owner, Bryan Rowntree, had her foredeck removed and seating installed, as the vessel is only used for day cruising. Beautifully restored, this vessel turns heads every time she is out of the boathouse. We have been unable to determine who was responsible for her design, but we should thank him.

Above: The 1936 *Alice* is a 24-foot triple cockpit runabout powered by an 8-cylinder Chrysler marine engine. Owned by Stan Meek, she has her home waters in Muskoka.

Opposite: The 1936 *Arequipa,* a 22-foot triple cockpit runabout offers proof positive that Ditchburn quality was still a priority of the builder. Owned by Ian Bruce, this beautiful vessel is on Lake of Bays.

Photo by Tom Thomson, Kenora, Ontario.

Right: A happy participant, Lindsey Hopkins of Atlanta, Georgia, enjoys the boats and people at the Muskoka show in Gravenhurst.

Opposite: The 20-foot *Top Hat*, a 1937 triple cockpit deluxe runabout, was trailered from Georgia to visit home waters in Muskoka. Restored in Florida, this streamlined hull carries the builder's plate 37-42, the third-from-last hull number recorded by Herb Ditchburn.

Above right: Miss Lindy is described in Herb Ditchburn's notes as a "special" runabout and most boaters would agree. Her hull number is 37-9 and she was launched in 1937 for Joseph E. Atkinson, longtime publisher of the *Toronto Star* newspaper. In his biography, Atkinson admitted that his favourite recreation was "driving a high-speedboat." He must have been a shrewd negotiator, as Ditchburn claims to have only made $8.05 on the transaction. Times were really tough for custom boat-builders.

Above left: A fold-down hatch cover covers the rear seat.

Below left: Power is supplied by a V-12 Scripps engine.

Opposite: The 40-foot cruiser *Duchess* carries hull number 37-3 and is the last Ditchburn cruiser built. Delivered to John Henry Molson in Montreal in May 1937, she spent her early years in Quebec waters. Acquired by Toronto owner Harvey Morris, she has been well maintained and extensively cruised on the Great Lakes.

Photos supplied by the owners of *Miss Lindy* and *Duchess.*

Chapter Nine

A HEROIC CONTRIBUTION TO WINNING THE WAR

*L*ike many production efforts clouded by wartime secrecy, this story has never been printed, and its telling provides vindication for Ditchburn's recognition as a boat-building genius.

Many friends and neighbours knew that Herb Ditchburn had moved to Trenton, Ontario, in 1940, to be involved in building boats for the war effort. Very few people have an appreciation of how extensive his contribution was, combining as it did all the experience and skills that he had accumulated in a lifetime as a builder and designer of boats. Like many production efforts clouded by wartime secrecy, this story has never been printed, and its telling provides vindication for his recognition as a boat-building genius.

The story actually begins in 1929, with the building of a 45-foot, ketch-rigged sailing yacht for Senator William Alexander Fraser, a prominent resident of Trenton, and a tireless champion for business improvement in the Bay of Quinte area. A few years before the outbreak of the Second World War, Senator Fraser had been successful in securing the establishment of the Trenton Air Force Base, which was to become a huge training complex in the Commonwealth Air Training Plan.

At the start of the war, Canada became a much-needed production resource for every imaginable war material, and contracts were readily available. Small vessels of every type were suddenly in demand. One particular contract came to the senator's attention, and he immediately thought of a solution. The British Air Ministry urgently required fast, seaworthy rescue boats for use in the English Channel, and Senator Fraser realized he knew the man who could build them.

Herb Ditchburn responded immediately to the call, moving to Trenton, where he lived for the rest of his life. Having built many vessels for government service, he understood the requirement and quickly designed an 80-foot vessel much like a motor torpedo boat. A company was incorporated, called Aero-Marine Crafts Ltd., involving Gar Wood and his brother Phil as directors. The Woods could supply the three Liberty engines needed for each vessel. These engines were modified aircraft engines,

Opposite: Portia **is the 45-foot ketch built for Senator Fraser in 1929.**

A sea trial of hospital ship 155 in the Bay of Quinte shows a fair turn of speed. One of six sister ships built by Aero-Marine Crafts Ltd., she was designed by Herb Ditchburn and powered with three Liberty engines provided by Gar Wood.

surplus from the First World War, but they had been used successfully for unlimited racing during the 1920s and 1930s. More modern engines were not available, being desperately needed for aircraft and tanks.

The design specifications were accepted and the contract awarded. In a small factory at the mouth of the Quinte River in Trenton Harbour, construction began on six of the 80-foot "hospital" ships, as the Air Ministry designated them. Their mission on delivery to England was crucial in the Battle of Britain. Their dangerous duty was to dash out into the channel during aerial warfare, rescuing aircrew that had been shot down or parachuted into the Channel. Trained pilots were in very short supply, and returning a pilot to active service as quickly as possible was a top priority. Since the English Channel is often an uncomfortable stretch of water, and German ships, aircraft, and shore batteries were plentiful, these small ships needed to be fast and manoeuvrable.

Built in record time and to the highest standards, these Ditchburn-designed warships were a credit to their builder. Senator Fraser had found the right man at the right time.

In 1942, a further order came along, but not for hospital ships—that phase of the war had been won. Now the requirement was for welded-steel harbour tugs, which were needed by the Royal Navy in almost every port in a war area, particularly in the Far East. The Central Bridge Construction Co. of Trenton, a company well skilled in steel construction, had never built a boat, but secured the order. Herb Ditchburn was requested by Senator Fraser to join the team and organize the construction of the 64-foot vessels.

While Herb Ditchburn had built over 1,000 boats in his lifetime, none had been in

steel. Two hundred highly skilled workers were available, so Herb's task was to organize this force into a production line. Huge problems faced the operation, but they were all overcome as methods were developed for every stage of construction.

Hulls were built upside down in the building, and then moved outside on completion.

Talking shop. Herb Ditchburn, of Trenton, left, and Hans Sachau, of Toronto, meet in 1943 to discuss war work. Ditchburn was building all-welded steel tugs; Sachau was building 112-foot wooden Fairmiles in his Humber Bay shop.

In the yard outside the Central Bridge Company building, engines, fittings, and superstructures were added to the completed hulls.

A sub-assembly line fabricated deckhouses and fittings, which were added to the hulls in the yard, along with a 240-horsepower Vivian diesel engine, a massive shaft, and a 1,500-pound propeller. Prefabrication was one of the principal features instituted by Ditchburn, and even the engine-room piping and electrical harnesses were being built in this manner. Each tug, when outfitted for firefighting and with the necessary equipment for harbour duties, weighed in at 74 tons. At first, the building process was uneven, but soon two vessels were being completed each week.

Since the factory was almost 2 miles from the nearest water, a specially built railway was necessary to get the finished tugs to the launch site at Trenton Harbour. After a test run in Lake Ontario, a representative of the British Ministry of War Transport passed the tug. Fleets of completed vessels were made up, travelling on their own bottoms across the lake to enter the barge canal at Oswego, then down the Hudson River to the port of Baltimore or New York for transport as deck cargo to various theatres of war.

Above: Workmen drive a massive shaft into the hull before fitting the 1,500-pound propeller.

Below: A crane barge in Baltimore Harbour prepares to lift a tug aboard a British freighter for delivery to some distant theatre of war.

A Young Boy with a Dream

When Herb Ditchburn took up residence in Trenton at the invitation of Senator Fraser, he became totally occupied by the requirements of the Canadian government for service vessels needed for the war. But he was not too busy to respond to the boating interest of a teenage nephew of the senator.

Eben James, now a senior citizen and lifelong boater, recalls their first meeting: "We were taken on a school tour of the Aero-Marine plant, set up in a vacant sawmill where the six high-speed hospital boats were being built. Mr. Ditchburn was in rolled-up shirt sleeves, going from worker to worker, checking their progress. Local carpenters were being taught to build these beautiful vessels in mahogany. I was enormously impressed.

"Later, I told my uncle of my interest to build a runabout for myself and he promised to speak to Mr. Ditchburn, who lived on the next street over. That night, I received a phone call from him saying he would love to be involved in the design and construction of a runabout. He invited me to come to his house where he had a drafting table set up. You could tell that he loved anything to do with boats.

"When our design was completed, my job was to procure the materials, which was difficult to do during the war. However, I gathered up oak, mahogany, and cedar and found a new 100-horsepower Mercury V-8 engine, so I was on my way. My father provided a workshop, and my major tool was a bandsaw. Mr. Ditchburn would come down evenings and Saturdays and show me how to fit planks, how to put in a double bottom, and fit other parts. He was very interested in the project, and I relished the time with him. We launched the boat together, put it through its paces, and he said, 'You know, young man, that is a good boat.'

"I was a young boy with a dream, and Mr. Ditchburn made that dream a reality. I will always remember that relationship with him. To this day, when I visit antique boat shows, Ditchburn boats are still considered the finest in design and craftsmanship."

Amateur boat-builder Eben James test drives his runabout built with design and construction advice from Herb Ditchburn. Photo courtesy Eben James.

An astonishing 260 tugs were built at this factory between 1942 and 1945. It was another case of the right man for the job. At war's end a citation of merit was presented to the company, expressing the government's admiration for this remarkable achievement. The citation stated in part: "The shipbuilding history of Canada would not be complete without recording the mass production of all-welded steel tugs for the British Navy by the Central Bridge Company of Trenton. A great many of these sturdy craft have been built and shipped for service in all parts of the world. None of their employees had any previous experience of steel ship construction, yet in the month of April 1944, this company launched 14 steel tugs complete for the British Navy in one day. The constant stream of such an important auxiliary being turned out by them will forever stand to their credit."

The townspeople of Trenton witness a tug launching in 1942.

Chapter Ten

REFLECTIONS

Ditchburn's products are still recognized as some of the best and most beautiful boats ever built in Canada. His important innovations in construction, mechanical systems, and design produced higher standards of customer satisfaction, safety, and utility. His vessels possessed a singular beauty—a sculptural quality that set them apart.

Herbert Ditchburn was born in Muskoka in 1880. He died in Trenton in 1950 and is buried in St. John's Anglican Cemetery there. It is a reflection of the quality of his life and his contribution to pleasure boating in Canada that this volume has been undertaken.

Apprenticed to his uncle Henry about the turn of the century, he learned boat building, soon bought out his uncle and grew with the company, acquiring skills in construction, design, and marketing. Over his career he built in excess of 1,000 vessels, ranging from rowboats to government patrol boats. His racing craft captured world titles for speed and endurance. He trained hundreds of employees in the skills required by the

company. He set the highest standards for his products, and he treated his customers with the utmost in fairness and respect. His integrity, skill, and artistry were represented in every vessel of his production.

Today his products are still recognized as some of the best and most beautiful boats ever built in Canada. His important innovations in construction, mechanical systems, and design produced higher standards of customer satisfaction, safety, and utility. His vessels possessed a singular beauty—a sculptural quality that set them apart.

Now his memory lives on, as collectors intend to preserve these Ditchburn treasures forever. Many Muskoka families have had a Ditchburn in the boathouse for three or four generations. It has become the ultimate cachet to own a Ditchburn, a masterwork from a master craftsman.

Left and opposite: Crumbling ruins of the Ditchburn factory mark the sad demise of a proud Canadian company.

RESTORATION

Like most manmade articles, wooden boats have a limited lifespan, a time that can be extended by careful use, dedicated maintenance, proper housing and professional assistance. Eventually, to some degree, replacement becomes necessary. The challenge becomes to undertake the necessary steps in a thoughtful manner, respecting the materials and construction methods used by the builder so that change is minimal and the integrity of the vessel is maintained.

Supporting Ditchburn owners are a group of restoration shops whose knowledge and skills are dedicated to maintaining the Ditchburn fleet as close as humanly possible to original appearance, construction, design and materials. We are indebted to these skillful builders—the success of their thoughtful efforts is reflected in many of the pages of this volume.

Dwight Boyd, Clarion Boats, Campbellford, Ontario

Peter Breen, Antique & Classic Boat Co. Ltd., Rockwood, Ontario

Tony Brown, Western Runabouts, Lake Tahoe, California

Tim Butson, Butson Boats Ltd., Port Carling, Ontario

Gary Clark, Clark Wooden Boats, Severn Bridge, Ontario

Ken Heshka, Canadian Heritage Boats, Winnipeg, Manitoba

Stan Hunter, Stan Hunter Boatbuilders, Port Carling, Ontario

Ken Lavalette, Woodwind Yachts, Nestleton, Ontario

Ed Skinner, Duke Marine Services, Port Carling, Ontario

Lance Wilson, Runabout Restorations, Umatilla, Florida

Mike Windsor, Windsor Boat Works Ltd., Gravenhurst, Ontario

A boatbuilder can learn much about the intricacies of wooden boat construction and sensitive restoration at Clark Wooden Boats near Severn Bridge, Ontario.

ACKNOWLEDGMENTS

Over the past two years, photographer Bev McMullen has spent hundreds of hours recording beautiful images of Ditchburn boats. She brought enormous talent and unending enthusiasm to this huge task, which was often complicated by uncooperative weather. She received the utmost cooperation from every owner, who gladly made every effort to assist her work. To these owners we offer our sincere thanks; it could never have happened without your help.

We would also like to recognize the special assistance provided by many others and thank them for being so helpful. Marion and Cyril Fry, honourary archivists of the Gravenhurst Public Library, provided access to their Ditchburn files, including a helpful monograph on the Ditchburn family by Cecil Porter.

Gail Ward, archivist of the Orillia Public Library, provided access to Orillia newspaper files of the period 1924–1932.

Bruce Wilson of Port Sandfield, a past owner of Greavette Boats Ltd., provided a carefully preserved and invaluable photographic collection from the sales records of Tom Greavette during his long career as sales manager of Ditchburn Boats.

Mrs. Irma Ditchburn of Toronto allowed access to personal papers, printed material, and photographs belonging to Herbert Ditchburn and passed to his son, Herbert Jr., now deceased. These records have now been donated to the Ontario Archives and will be available in the near future when they have been properly accessioned. Historical material on the life of T. J. Ditchburn is from the archives of the Mariners' Musuem, Newport News, Virginia, and is supplied by Mrs. Irma Ditchburn. Catalogue illustrations of canoes, rowing boats, and early motorboats are from original printed material of the Ditchburn company and are supplied by Mrs. Irma Ditchburn.

Murray Walker and John Blair provided several useful references from *Canadian Power Boating* magazines of the 1930s. Brian O'Meara, managing editor of the *Trentonian* newspaper in Trenton, provided files and photographs of the hospital boats built by Aero-Marine Crafts Ltd. History of *Grace Anne II* and photographs on pages 82–83, and 114, provided by Salisbury Cruises Ltd., Kenora, Ontario. The Trenton Public Library provided photographs taken by the National Film Board in 1944 of the construction of steel harbour tugs by Central Bridge Co.

Eben James, nephew of Senator William A. Fraser, provided invaluable assistance in the research into Herb Ditchburn's outstanding and largely unrecognized contribution in Trenton to the war effort. He also provided a recollection of his personal relationship with Herb Ditchburn, which offers an enjoyable insight.

To these persons and many others, Bev and I are extremely grateful.